BREAK THE LANGUAGE BARRIER LEVEL 4
WWW.ELPRINCIPECENTRE.COM
info@elprincipecentre.com

INTRODUCTION

If you have chosen this book to help you learn Spanish you will have either already completed Levels 1, 2 and/ or 3 or will have felt that your level of Spanish was sufficient to start here at Level 4. Level 4 assumes knowledge and confidence with present and past and future tenses in all aspects and I would not recommend starting this course without this.

If you find difficulty from the beginning, it would be a good idea to start with Level 1, 2 or 3 for the good foundations they will give you. Here in Level 4 we will continue to practice the past and future tenses and learn to begin to tackle the mysterious and difficult to grasp subjunctive. My method of teaching Spanish is all about communication rather than grammatical perfection.

However, I do not advocate "phrasebook" Spanish or "holiday" Spanish. With my method you will learn how to take the various components of the language in the simplest form possible and build your own phrases and questions to leave you confident in any situation. Spanish is a lovely, rich language spoken widely throughout the world. Most importantly, I hope you will enjoy working through this Level and feel sufficiently confident at the end to cope with anything. The subjunctive is a ethereal and puzzling tense to English speakers, a concept alien to us and therefore very difficult to learn. I personally steadfastly ignored it for years and I found eventually that the best way to use it was to forget trying to understand it and instead concentrate on the phrases and expressions that provoke it so that you are using it instinctively.

Languages do not always have logical explanations that what makes them fun at the same time as being intensely annoying. We always have to remember that they were spoken first for centuries and written down and made sense of later not the other way around and that is why the grammar doesn´t always have a rational explanation. "Solo porque" is often the best explanation we have!! ☺

Suerte!!
Vicki

Copyright© Vicki Marie Riley 2021. All rights reserved.

BREAK THE LANGUAGE BARRIER LEVEL 4
WWW.ELPRINCIPECENTRE.COM
info@elprincipecentre.com

INDEX	Page No.
1. INTRODUCE YOURSELF	4
2. TRANSLATION AND COMPREHENSION PRACTICE WITH VARIOUS TENSES, ENGLISH TO SPANISH	5
3. THE PRESENT SUBJUNCTIVE 1- FORMATION AND EXPRESSIONS OF DESIRE.	8
4. THE PRESENT SUBJUNCTIVE 2- DOUBT OR IGNORANCE	9
5. THE PRESENT SUBJUNCTIVE 3- IMPERSONAL OPINION	13
6. THE PRESENT SUBJUNCTIVE 4 - UNCOMPLETED ACTION	15
7. THE PRESENT SUBJUNCTIVE 5- INDEFINITE OBJECT	17
8. THE PRESENT SUBJUNCTIVE 6- "QUIZÁ" AND "AUNQUE"	19
9. COPPPRINCT AND FLOMMETS REVISITED.	21
10. THE PRESENT SUNBJUNCTIVE- "SER" AND "ESTAR"	21
11. PRACTICE THE PRESENT SUBJUNCTIVE	22
12. CONVERSATION PRACTICE PRESENT SUBJUNCTIVE	26
13. PRESENT SUBJUNCTIVE IN CONTEXT- DEAR RICHARD	27
14. DOLOR DE MUELAS	29
15. THE IMPERFECT SUBJUNCTIVE	33
16. PRACTICE THE PAST SUBJUNCTIVE	36
17. VIAJE A ESPAÑA	37
18. THE PAST SUBJUNCTIVE- "SER" AND "ESTAR"	39
19. ONE SUNDAY MORNING	42
20. VERB TABLES	43
21. FINISH THE STORY	55
22. ADJECTIVE PRONOUNS	56
23. TRANSLATION ENGLISH TO SPANISH - THE GARDENER	60
24. TRANSLATION ENGLISH TO SPANISH- THE COOK	61
25. COMMON VERBS THAT TAKE PREPOSITIONS	62
26. ORDINAL NUMBERS	65
27. AT THE DOCTORS	66
28. THE GENERATION "DINK"	67
29. POSTSCRIPT	68
30. KEY TO "TOP TIPS	69
31. ANSWER KEY	70

Copyright© Vicki Marie Riley 2021. All rights reserved.

BREAK THE LANGUAGE BARRIER LEVEL 4
WWW.ELPRINCIPECENTRE.COM
info@elprincipecentre.com

1. INTRODUCE YOURSELF.

If you are ready for Level 4, you should be able to ask and answer the following questions in Spanish. If you have problems with these, please go back through Levels 1, 2 and 3 to refresh before starting this course.

DINOS ALGO SOBRE TÍ...

1. Where did you work before?
2. Why and when did you come to Spain?
3. Do you have any children?
4. What is your partner like?
5. Will you go on holiday next year?
6. Would you live in another country?
7. How have you practised Spanish since your last class?
8. How are you going to practise after this book?
9. How long have you studied Spanish?
10. What did you do last weekend?
11. Would you speak to a stranger on a train?
12. What are the biggest problems that you have had in learning Spanish?
13. What do you want to achieve after this book?
14. Have you bought a new car this year?
15. When was the last time that you spoke Spanish?
16. How many languages do you speak?
17. When is your birthday?
18. What did you do on your birthday last year?
19. Where did you live when you were a child?
20. Would you be happy living in Spain?

Copyright© Vicki Marie Riley 2021. All rights reserved.

BREAK THE LANGUAGE BARRIER LEVEL 4
WWW.ELPRINCIPECENTRE.COM
info@elprincipecentre.com

2. TRANSLATION AND COMPREHENSION PRACTICE WITH VARIOUS TENSES, ENGLISH TO SPANISH- ME HABÍAN ROBADO.

The other day **_I was walking_** along the street when suddenly someone pushed me and I found myself on the floor without realising it. At first, I was so shocked that I started to shout like an idiot. Then I realised that I hadn't hurt myself, but when I put my hand in my trouser pocket, I discovered that I had been robbed. Many people approached me to ask me if I needed help.

I said that my wallet had been stolen and a boy said that he had seen someone run along the street and that without doubt it was the thief. As soon as he had said this, he began to run in that direction. After a while, he returned saying that he had seen the thief and that that they had followed him for a good while, but that suddenly he had disappeared into a side street.

I wanted to thank him, so we went to a café and I bought him a drink with the few euros I was carrying loose in my pocket. Then I went to a Police Station to make a statement that I had been robbed. In my wallet, besides the money, which wasn't much, I was also carrying my identity card, my driving licence, and my credit cards.

PRACTICE A: Pick out the 39 verbs in this text and use them to complete the verb identification table below. The first one has been done for you.

VERB	INFINITIVE	SPANISH	TENSE	PERSON
1. I was walking	To walk	andar	imperfecto	1st sing
2.				
3.				
4.				
5.				
6.				
7.				
8.				
9.				
10.				
11.				
12.				
13.				

Copyright© Vicki Marie Riley 2021. All rights reserved.

14.				
15.				
16.				
17.				
18.				
19.				
20.				
21.				
22.				
23.				
24.				
25.				
26.				
27.				
28.				
29.				
30.				
31.				
32.				
33.				
34.				
35.				
36.				
37.				
38.				
39.				

PRACTICE B: Translate the text into Spanish.

PRACTICE C: Re-write the translation in the 3rd **person singular**.
E.g. The other day **he was walking** down the street when suddenly someone pushed **him** etc, etc.

PRACTICE D: Make 10 questions about the text to ask your classmates in Spanish.

Copyright© Vicki Marie Riley 2021. All rights reserved.

BREAK THE LANGUAGE BARRIER LEVEL 4
WWW.ELPRINCIPECENTRE.COM
info@elprincipecentre.com

Top Tips!!

1. VERBS THAT CHANGE MEANING IN THE PRETERITE TENSE

1.1.

CONOCER- Present tense- To know a person or a place.
E.g. **Conozco** a Juan: I **know** Juan
But
Preterite tense- to meet
Eg **Conocí** a Juan en 2010: I **met** Juan in 2010

PODER- Present tense- to "can" or be able.
E.g. ¿**Puedes** abrir la ventana?: **Can** you open the window?
But
Preterite tense-(positive) to manage to/(negative) to fail to
E.g. ¿**Pudiste** abrir la ventana?: Did you **manage to** open the window?
No **pude** abrir la ventana: I **failed** to open the window.

QUERER- Present tense- To want or to love.
E.g. **Quieren** comprar un coche nuevo: They **want** to buy a new car.
But
Preterite tense- (positive) to try/ negative to refuse.
E.g. **Quisieron** comprar el coche: They **wanted** to buy the car.
No **quisieron** comprar el coche: They **refused** to buy the car.

SABER- Present tense- to know facts or information
E.g **Saben** la verdad: They **know** the truth
But
Preterite tense- to find out
E.g. **Supieron** la verdad: They **found out** the truth.

Copyright© Vicki Marie Riley 2021. All rights reserved.

BREAK THE LANGUAGE BARRIER LEVEL 4
WWW.ELPRINCIPECENTRE.COM
info@elprincipecentre.com

3. THE PRESENT SUBJUNCTIVE 1- FORMATION AND EXPRESSIONS OF DESIRE.

1. FORMATION

Almost all verbs are formed in the same way:

Take the 1st person singular of the simple present:

E.g. **como, vivo, hablo, conozco, tengo, hago, quiero, salgo, veo**

Then remove the "o" and add back the following endings:

-"ar" verbs- e,es,e,emos,éis,en
-"er" and "ir" verbs- a,as,a,amos,áis,an

E.g. **hable, hables, hable, hablemos, habléis, hablen
tenga, tengas, tenga, tengamos, tengáis, tengan
viva, vivas, viva, vivamos, viváis, vivan**

There are a few irregular verbs as follows:

**Dar- dé, des, dé, demos, deis, den
Estar- esté, estés, esté, estemos, estéis, esten
Haber- haya, hayas, haya, hayamos, hayáis, hayan
Ir- vaya, vayas, vaya, vayamos, vayáis, vayan
Saber- sepa, sepas, sepa, sepamos, sepáis, sepan
Ser- sea, seas, sea, seamos, seáis, sean**

You will use the subjunctive to express certain things, normally in a sentence of 2 clauses.

The two sentences are often separated by **"que"-that**. In this first subjunctive module we will look at **EXPRESSIONS OF DESIRE**.

Copyright© Vicki Marie Riley 2021. All rights reserved.

BREAK THE LANGUAGE BARRIER LEVEL 4
WWW.ELPRINCIPECENTRE.COM
info@elprincipecentre.com

1. EXPRESSIONS OF DESIRE

PRACTICE A: These are commonly used verbs and expressions of desire that trigger the use of the subjunctive. Find their meanings.

1. Esperar -
2. Exigir -
3. Insistir en -
4. Ojalá -
5. Pedir -
6. Preferir -
7. Querer -
8. Rogar -
9. Sugerir –

PRACTICE B: Use them to translate the examples below into English.

EXAMPLES:

1. Prefiero que cogáis el autobús.
2. Insisten en que tenga yo la casa.
3. Quieres que te amen mucho.
4. Espero que puedan bailar bien.
5. Pide que te sientes ahora.
6. Esperan que viva ella en aquella casa.

PRACTICE C: Translate into Spanish.

Remember it is the verb in the SECOND CLAUSE that takes the subjunctive

1. I hope that she calls me tomorrow.
2. He wants you to eat the sandwich.
3. They want us to write a letter.
4. We hope that you are well.
5. She wants us to do it.
6. I insist that they do it.
7. We suggest that you try it.
8. They always insist that I work with them.
9. He requests that we arrive at 9 o´clock.

Copyright© Vicki Marie Riley 2021. All rights reserved.

10. They prefer that we leave on Friday.
11. I hope that you know them.
12. We insist that you eat lunch with us.
13. Do you want me to count the money?
14. I suggest that we all leave now.
15. They suggest that we put the money in the bank.

PRACTICE D: Translate into Spanish. Verbs that take the subjunctive are in italics. Note that often in English we use the infinitive rather than the subjunctive.

Tomorrow is the first day of my daughter´s new life. I hope that everything **goes** well for her. My new son-in-law seems very nice, but I prefer that he **is** more honest than friendly. I want him **to always show** her love and respect. I want him **to tell** me directly how he will improve the life of my daughter. I´m going to request that he always **tells** her the truth. If he suggests that I **don´t help** her with the children I will be very sad.

Top Tips!!

2. SOME "FALSE FRIENDS" THAT DON´T MEAN WHAT YOU THINK

EMBARAZADA- PREGNANT
LA CARPETA- THE FOLDER
ESTAR CONSTIPADO- TO HAVE A COLD
EL DELITO- THE CRIME
EL PRESERVATIVO- CONDOM
MOLESTAR- TO ANNOY
DECEPCIONAR- TO DISAPPOINT
ONCE- ELEVEN
LA MAMA- BREAST
EL ÉXITO- SUCCESS

BREAK THE LANGUAGE BARRIER LEVEL 4
WWW.ELPRINCIPECENTRE.COM
info@elprincipecentre.com

4. THE PRESENT SUBJUNCTIVE 2- DOUBT OR IGNORANCE.
(Refer to chapter 3 for formation of the subjunctive.)

If there is a verb in the main clause of a sentence that expresses ignorance or doubt it will set up the need for the subjunctive in the second clause.

PRACTICE A: Below are some commonly used expressions that provoke the need for the subjunctive. Find their meanings:

1. Dudar que-
2. No creer que-
3. No estar convencido/a de que-
4. No estar seguro/a de que-
5. No imaginarse que-
6. No parecer que-
7. No pensar que-
8. No suponer que-
9. Temer que-

PRACTICE B: Use them to translate these examples into English.

1. Dudo que vengan.
2. Temen que sea demasiado tarde.
3. No parece que estén aquí.
4. No te imaginas que tengan buenas intenciones.
5. No creemos que vayamos a Inglaterra en Junio.
6. No pienso que él quiera ir.

PRACTICE C- Translate into Spanish.

1. We doubt that they work in that factory.
2. I don´t suppose that they will tell me the truth.
3. He doesn´t believe that I am happy.
4. I´m not sure they will go.
5. They don´t think that food will be ready.
6. We are not convinced that you(s) know us.
7. Why doesn´t he believe that you are honest?

Copyright© Vicki Marie Riley 2021. All rights reserved.

8. She doubts that we know the answer.
9. They´re not sure that we always arrive on time.
10. Why aren´t you convinced that it will work well?
11. It doesn´t seem that he wants to go.
12. We´re not sure that she can do this.
13. She doesn´t believe that we are together.
14. Don´t you(s) imagine that it is all true.

PRACTICE D- Translate into Spanish. (Verbs in italics take the present subjunctive)

I doubt that David **knows** that I am planning a surprise for him. It doesn´t seem possible that he **is** nearly 50, and I don´t imagine that he **believes** it either. I don´t suppose that he **is expecting** a party and I doubt that he **likes** all the attention. I´m not convinced that **he will be** happy. However, I don´t suppose that he **will say** anything. I just want everything **to go** well for him.

Top Tips!!

3. COMMON VERBS MY STUDENTS CONFUSE:

LLEGAR/ LLEVAR/ LAVAR- TO ARRIVE/ TO WEAR/TAKE/ TO WASH
PONER/ PODER- TO PUT/ TO BE ABLE
HACER/TENER- TO DO/MAKE/ TO HAVE
HABER/TENER- TO HAVE (DONE)/ TO HAVE (POSSESSION)
COMER/ ALMORZAR- TO HAVE LUNCH/ TO HAVE ELEVENSES
(NOTE THAT ALMORZAR IS USED FOR LUNCH IN LATIN AMERICAN SPANISH COUNTRIES BUT NEVER IN SPAIN)

5. THE PRESENT SUBJUNCTIVE 3- IMPERSONAL OPINION.

(Refer to chapter 3 for formation of the subjunctive)

An impersonal opinion, (ie not referring to any specific person), in the main clause of a sentence will set up the need for the subjunctive in the second clause.

PRACTICE A- Below are some commonly used impersonal expressions which provoke the need for the subjunctive. Find their meanings:

1. Conviene que-
2. Es fantastico que-
3. Es importante que-
4. Es imposible que-
5. Es improbable que-
6. Es increíble que-
7. Es una lastíma que-
8. Es mejor que-
9. Es necesario que-
10. Es posible que-
11. Es probable que-
12. Es preferible que-
13. Es ridículo que-
14. Es terrible que-
15. Más vale que-
16. Ojalá que-
17. Puede ser que-

PRACTICE B- Translate the examples below into English.

1. Es una lástima que no pueda ir yo.
2. Es ridículo que no puedan hacerlo.
3. Es terrible que él no tenga trabajo.
4. Es necesario que aprendas el subjunctivo para hablar bien el español.
5. Ojalá que no nos despertemos tarde.
6. Es mejor que no digas nada.

BREAK THE LANGUAGE BARRIER LEVEL 4
WWW.ELPRINCIPECENTRE.COM
info@elprincipecentre.com

PRACTICE C: Translate into Spanish.

1. It´s better that we don´t drink alcohol.
2. It is advisable that you close the windows.
3. It´s preferable that you don´t eat meat.
4. It´s unlikely that she will want to go.
5. It´s necessary that you take an interpreter with you.
6. It´s important that no one knows the truth.
7. It may be that they live in a different city now.
8. It´s ridiculous that so many children can´t spell.
9. It´s impossible that we finish the job this week.
10. It´s incredible that she speaks 7 languages.
11. It´s a shame that wine is so expensive in Great Britain.
12. It´s fantastic that I have so many friends.
13. It may be that David is tall and good-looking.
14. It´s impossible that we stay in England all summer.
15. If only they had more time.

PRACTICE A: Translate the text. Verbs in italics need the subjunctive.

Last night I went to the cinema for the first time. It´s possible that *I am* the only person that has never been. There are so many silly reasons. For example, it´s ridiculous that *I am* so nervous of public places. It´s better that a person *has* the freedom to leave at any moment if that is what he or she needs to do. Also, it´s incredible that *we have to* sit next to strangers in the cinema, that is very difficult for me. It´s better that *we sit* apart from other people but I know this is impossible. If only *I didn´t have* all these silly phobias.

Copyright© Vicki Marie Riley 2021. All rights reserved.

6. THE PRESENT SUBJUNCTIVE 4 - UNCOMPLETED ACTION.

(Refer to chapter 3 for formation of the subjunctive)

When the action in the subordinate clause of a sentence is indefinite or pending, (i.e hasn´t happened yet), this provokes the need for the subjunctive.

PRACTICE A: Find the English meanings of these commonly used connecting phrases which provoke the need for the subjunctive.

1. A menos que-
2. Antes de que-
3. Con tal que-
4. Cuando-
5. Después de que-
6. En caso de que-
7. Hasta que-
8. Mientras que-
9. Para que-
10. Sin que-
11. Tan pronto como-

PRACTICE B: Translate these examples:

1. Te llamaré tan pronto como llegue.
2. No iremos a menos que vayas tú.
3. Estudio mucho en caso de que haya un examen.
4. Trabajo para que podamos comer.
5. Tocará el piano con tal de que cantéis vosotros.
6. Viviré aquí hasta que tenga otra casa.
7. Estudiamos el subjuntivo para que lo entendamos mejor.
8. José prepara la ensalada mientras que yo haga la paella.
9. No comeré la paella sin que la comas tú también.
10. Cuando podáis, traedme los papeles.
11. Nos vamos a casa después de que nos traigan la cuenta.

PRACTICE C: Translate these sentences

BREAK THE LANGUAGE BARRIER LEVEL 4
WWW.ELPRINCIPECENTRE.COM
info@elprincipecentre.com

1. I won´t eat until I´m hungry.
2. I have written you a note so that you remember to buy milk.
3. You will feel better after you take this medicine.
4. He wont marry a woman unless she is rich.
5. I´ll dry the dishes while you wash them.
6. I´ll believe it when I see it.
7. We will ring him again in case he forgets.
8. They won´t buy anything unless it is cheap.
9. Every day she takes a tablet so she doesn´t get ill.
10. You must brush your teeth before we go to the dentists.
11. You(s) can´t help him until he changes his life.
12. Can you do this homework when you have the time.
13. They don´t go to the doctors without they make an appointment first.
14. She will close the door after she enters the room.
15. We will speak lots of Spanish as soon as we understand the subjunctive.

PRACTICE D: Translate this short text. Subjunctive verbs are in italics.

David promises that he will call me as soon as **he gets there.** However, he will probably only call when *isn´t* busy with work. I think that he will tell me all about it when **he arrives home**. He won´t call unless a miracle **happens**. He could call me while he *is* on the train, but he won´t do that in case **he misses** something interesting. He will call provided that **I call** him often and tell him that I want him **to come back**. We will be happy after **he finishes** work.

Copyright© Vicki Marie Riley 2021. All rights reserved.

BREAK THE LANGUAGE BARRIER LEVEL 4
WWW.ELPRINCIPECENTRE.COM
info@elprincipecentre.com

7. THE PRESENT SUBJUNCTIVE 5- INDEFINITE OBJECT
(Refer to chapter 3 for formation of the subjunctive)

When the object of the main clause in a sentence is indefinite, (i.e. isn't known to actually exist), it provokes the need for the subjunctive.

For example, if I said:

"I have a house that has 3 bedrooms" the house ia real so it would translate to **"Tengo una casa que tiene 3 dormitorios"**.

However, if I said:

"I am looking for a house that has three bedrooms", the house so far hasn't been found so would provoke the use of the subjunctive: **"Busco una casa que tenga 3 dormitorios"**.

PRACTICE A: Translate into English.

1. Preferimos un país que tenga mucha vida
2. Buscan un perro que no ladre mucho.
3. Necesita un piso que tenga ascensor.
4. No hay nadie en la casa que tenga la llave.
5. Queremos un restaurante que venda tapas.
6. Busco una peluquera que sepa cortar pelo bien.
7. Ella quiere marido que sea rico.
8. Debe estar alguien aqui que conozca yo.
9. Para mi cumpleaños quiero un anillo que tenga un diamante enorme.
10. Todos queremos un niño que este contento.

PRACTICE B: Translate into Spanish.

1. We are looking for a secretary that is efficient.
2. They want a job that pays a lot of money.
3. Are there any shops around here that sell stamps?
4. You need a car that won't cost much.
5. Is there anybody here that speaks Spanish?

6. Carlos is looking for a school that teaches French.
7. I want a skirt that is long and red.
8. There isn't anyone here that can help you.
9. For my birthday I want a mobile telephone that takes photos.
10. I want to live in a world where there is no poverty.
11. Is there anyone here that has a pen?
12. They need someone who works hard.
13. He is looking for a sofa that has 3 seats.
14. They need a friend that lives nearby.
15. We want a hotel room that has a good view.

PRACTICE C: Translate this short text. Subjunctive verbs are in italics.

I went on holiday with my friend last month. I will never go with her again. She wants too much. First, she wants a hotel that *is* very close to the beach. Then she wants a room that *is* on the ground floor but *has* a sea view. She also wants a hotel that *looks* expensive but she wants this hotel to *cost* less than 200 euros for a week. She wants meals that *are* tasty and cocktails that *have* a lot of alcohol. I told her that there is no hotel in Spain that *provides* all these things for 200 euros. In fact, I said there is no one in the world that *understands* her demands.

Top Tips!!

4. MOST COMMON MISTAKES MY STUDENTS MAKE

In the fifteen-plus years I have been teaching Spanish, the same mistakes come up over and over again in class from my students. Here are some of them:

- Confusing "su" and "tu"- "su" is his, her or their, not "your".
- In Spanish we speak "with" people not "to" them- "hablar con" not "a".
- We use the verb "to do" or "make" to talk about the weather, not "to be".
- In a question, the verb always precedes the person.
- In a question, if there is a prepostion, it comes FIRST. (with, from, etc)

8. THE PRESENT SUBJUNCTIVE 6- "PERHAPS AND ALTHOUGH"-"QUIZÁ Y AUNQUE"

(Refer to previous module for formation of the subjunctive)

Phrases using **"quizá"** (meaning **"perhaps"** or **"maybe"**) or **"aunque"** (meaning **"although"** or **"even if"**) usually require the use of the subjunctive. However, **"aunque"** only provokes the need for the subjunctive if the action referred to hasn´t happened yet.

E.g
Even though it <u>may</u> be difficult, I will go
Aunque **sea** dificil, iré. (subjunctive) BUT

Although it <u>is</u> difficult, I will go
Aunque <u>es</u> dificil, iré. (present simple)

PRACTICE A: Translate into English.

1. Quizá no vaya yo mañana.
2. Aunque llueva, voy a la fiesta.
3. Quizá esten enfermos.
4. Aunque no hable francés, vive en Francia.
5. Quizá me quiera, pero no es muy valiente.
6. Aunque no me gusten los gatos, no los hago daño.
7. Quizá estemos más felices ahora.
8. Aunque sea cruel, le amo de todas formas.
9. Quizá trabajéis demasiado.
10. Aunque no te compremos el coche, alguien te lo comprará.

PRACTICE B: Translate into Spanish.

1. Maybe he has the money.
2. Even if Carlos goes, I won´t stay.
3. Although they may want to watch television, they can´t.
4. Although you may think you are ugly, everyone knows you are handsome.
5. Even if you shout at them, they won´t change.
6. Maybe we are idiots.

7. Perhaps we can go.
8. Although I may know the truth, I won´t tell you.
9. Even if you run, you won´t catch the bus.
10. Maybe they will buy the house today.
11. Even if he is ill, he has to work.
12. Perhaps we will live in America one day.
13. Even if you want to go, you can´t.
14. Although they may call, I don´t want to speak to them.
15. Even if I say yes, it is too late now.

PRACTICE B: The following text has examples of all the times we use the subjunctive we have studied. This time they are <u>not</u> highlighted. Good luck!!

There isn´t anyone who is good company as my boyfriend David. It´s great that he is coming to Spain this weekend as I haven´t seen him for two weeks. I hope that he makes his famous prawn cocktail again, but I doubt that he will make it this weekend because he made it last time. Even if he doesn´t prepare this dish, he will prepare something tasty. Maybe I will ask him, so that he buys the special prawns when he arrives. I hope that he says yes.

9. COPPPRINCT AND FLOMMETS REVISITED

"SER" - "COPPPRINCT"

C OLOURS
O RIGIN
P ROFESSION
P OSSESSION
P ERSONAL
R ELATIONSHIPS
I DENTITY
N ATIONALITY
C HARACTERISTICS
T IME

"ESTAR" - "FLOMMETS"

F EELINGS
L
O CATION
M OODS
M ARITAL STATUS
E MOTIONS
T EMPORARY
S TATES

Copyright© Vicki Marie Riley 2021. All rights reserved.

10. PRESENT SUBJUNCTIVE- "SER" AND "ESTAR".

SER	ESTAR
sea	esté
seas	estés
sea	esté
seamos	estemos
seáis	estéis
sean	estén

The subjunctive is always used with the following phrases/expressions:

1. esperar que
2. ojalá que
3. querer que
4. no creer que
5. no parecer que
6. dudar que
7. es imposible que
8. es necesario que
9. hasta que
10. cuando
11. tan pronto como
12. quizá
13. tal vez
14. aunque

PRACTICE A: Find out what these expressions mean and then use them to translate the sentences below. One from each group uses "SER" the other "ESTAR". Refer to "copprinct" and "flommets" on the previous page to decide which verb to use.

1. I hope that he isn't ill.
   I hope that he is handsome

2. God willing our neighbours will be Spanish
   God willing our neighbours won't be in the house.

3. Do you want me to be a nurse?
   Do you want me to be there with you?

4. I don't think she will be happy
   I don't think she will be tall

5. It doesn't seem it will be a good party.
   It doesn't seem it will be open.

BREAK THE LANGUAGE BARRIER LEVEL 4
WWW.ELPRINCIPECENTRE.COM
info@elprincipecentre.com

6. We doubt that they are very nice.
   We doubt that the banks are open at this time.

7. I can't go until it is open.
   I can't go until it is winter.

8. As soon as it is night I will go.
   As soon as it is open I will go.

9. Perhaps they will be tall, dark and handsome.
   Perhaps they will be in the bar.

10. Even if she is a nurse, I don't like her.
    Even if she is ill, I have no time for her.

11. It´s impossible that they are friends.
    It´s impossible that they are in the country.

12. It is necessary that we are always polite.
    It is necessary that we are always there with them.

13. When you are a doctor, I will call you.
    When you are in Spain, you will call me.

14. Maybe I will be a singer one day.
    Maybe I will be tired on Friday after work.

15. I don´t believe that I am a good singer.
    I don´t believe that I thay are married.

16. They will wait until he is here.
    They will wait until he is older.

17. We don't want you to be sad.
    We don't want you to be a doctor.

18. You(s) will go back to work as soon as you(s) are better.
    You(s) will know as soon as it is the right time.

Copyright© Vicki Marie Riley 2021. All rights reserved.

11. PRACTICE THE PRESENT SUBJUNCTIVE

PRACTICE A: Complete the following with true sentences about your actions, opinions, hopes and desires on any subject.

1. Deseo que....
2. Ojalá que....
3. No quiero que....
4. Aconsejo que...
5. No creo que...
6. Es posible que...
7. Me gustaría que...
8. Me parece ridículo que....
9. Ahorro dinero para que....
10. Es mejor que...
11. No pienso que..
12. Cuando estoy en mi casa, prefiero que...
13. En un restaurante, siempre espero que...
14. Pido que mis vecinos no....
15. En caso de emergencia en el coche, sugiero que...

PRACTICE B: Translate these sentences into Spanish, deciding whether to use the Present Simple or Subjunctive. (Notice that in some of the English sentences the future is used).

1. My friends say that this year it will not snow.
2. The doctor does not consider that the patient is walking well.
3. It is possible that we will need more hours to study.
4. Do you think it is possible that there will be 20 degrees in Murcia in December?
5. All the theories together are not capable of explaing this.
6. The streets are not wide, but perhaps this will be because there is no space.
7. It is good that we all communicate well.
8. Why oh why do we have to use the subjunctive?
9. I want a receptionist that speaks English And Spanish.
10. The receptionist at the doctors speaks five different languages.
11. She says that he is a good person.
12. We don´t believe that she is a very good person.

BREAK THE LANGUAGE BARRIER LEVEL 4
WWW.ELPRINCIPECENTRE.COM
info@elprincipecentre.com

Top Tips!!

5. SLANG EXPRESSIONS TO MAKE YOU SOUND LIKE A SPANIARD

- Ser la caña- To be awesome
- Chulo/a- cool (things), cocky (people)
- Ser la leche- dual meaning- To be really great or really awful!!
- Tener mala pata- To have bad luck
- Ir a tapear- To go for tapas
- Ser un pesado- to be a pain (person)
- Tio/tia- guy/ girl
- Colega- friend (male or female)
- Estar en pelotas- to be naked
- Guay- cool
- Estar como una cabra- to be crazy
- Perder los papeles- to lose the plot
- Andar con cien ojos- to keep your eyes open
- Pasarlo pipa/ bomba- To have a great time
- Hay tres gatos- There's no one here
- Valer la pena- to be worth it
- Dar la lata- to annoy/ irritate
- Echar la siesta- to have a siesta
- La marcha- nightlife
- Ojo- watch out
- Viejo verde- dirty old man
- Pijo/a- snob

Try making some sentences in the different tenses you have learned.
See the reaction you get when you use them to a Spanish speaker!!

Copyright© Vicki Marie Riley 2021. All rights reserved.

BREAK THE LANGUAGE BARRIER LEVEL 4
WWW.ELPRINCIPECENTRE.COM
info@elprincipecentre.com

12. CONVERSATION PRACTICE PRESENT SUBJUNCTIVE.

PRACTICE A: TRANSLATE THESE QUESTIONS INTO SPANISH AND ANSWER IN SPANISH

1. Would you make a barbecue at the weekend even if it rains?

2. Is it important to you that your friends are honest?

3. Dont you think that Spain is better that your country?

4. Do you take the duvet off your bed as soon as summer arrives?

5. Do you doubt that it will be hot this summer in Spain?

6. Do problems normally go away even if you dont do anything?

7. Is it impossible that you learn the subjunctive?

8. It doesn´t seem that the weather will be good on Sunday, do you still plan to go out?

9. Would you like to have a house that has more bedrooms than yours?

10. Would you like to buy a car that goes very fast?

11. What Spanish classes will you do after you learn the subjunctive?

12. Do you like restaurants that sell tapas?

13. Is there anywhere in your area that does Spanish classes?

14. Would you go on a cruise even if it was very expensive?

Copyright© Vicki Marie Riley 2021. All rights reserved.

BREAK THE LANGUAGE BARRIER LEVEL 4
WWW.ELPRINCIPECENTRE.COM
info@elprincipecentre.com

13. PRESENT SUBJUNCTIVE IN CONTEXT.

3rd of January.
Dear Richard

How **are** you? I hope that you are all well and I wish that New Year brings you all kinds of good things and that you see all your dreams realized. I hope that you forgive my long silence, but I have had practically no time to write to you. The reason for writing to you is that you would reserve for me, from the 21st of January, a single room in a good hotel that is near the city centre. It doesn't matter if it is expensive.

The most likely is that I will have to spend a few months in your country, as my company wants me to make a study of the possibility of opening a branch there. If you want me to tell you the truth, at first I wasn´t happy with the idea of having to be away from home for a long time, but now I am happy with the idea of having to be away from home for a long time, but now I am happy it will be like this, as it is a good opportunity for us to see each other again, and perhaps it will be a positive experience for my professional future.

I look forward to seeing you soon
Hugs

María.

PRACTICE A: Pick out the 32 verbs in this text and use them to complete the verb identification table below as per the example.

	VERB	INFINITIVE	SPANISH	TENSE	PERSON
1.					
2.					
3.					
4.					
5.					
6.					

Copyright© Vicki Marie Riley 2021. All rights reserved.

7.				
8.				
9.				
10.				
11.				
12.				
13.				
14.				
15.				
16.				
17.				
18.				
19.				
20.				
21.				
22.				
23.				
24.				
25.				
26.				
27.				
28.				
29.				
30.				
31.				
32.				

PRACTICE B: Translate the text into Spanish.

PRACTICE C: Write a similar email to a friend asking them to rent a flat for you near the beach for the summer months. Explain to them your price range, the location you require, how many bedrooms, dates etc. Try to use at least 3 examples of the present subjunctive.

BREAK THE LANGUAGE BARRIER LEVEL 4
WWW.ELPRINCIPECENTRE.COM
info@elprincipecentre.com

14. DOLOR DE MUELAS

Carmen tiene dolor de muelas pero no quiere que sepa su marido. No quiere ir a ver el dentista porque tiene miedo, aunque sea un hombre simpático. Por fin no puede aguantar más el dolor y habla con su hermano Pepe. Él dice que puede ser que la farmacia tenga algo para aliviar el dolor. **(16 verbos)**

Carmen va a la farmacia de la esquina. Está bastante llena de gente, y mientras el dependiente les sirve, Carmen mira todas las botellas y cajas en el mostrador buscando un remedio. Claro que no lo encuentra. Explica al dependiente lo del dolor de muelas y le pide consejo. Él se sonríe.
-No puedo ayudarte mucho. Conviene que vayas al dentista lo antes posible. Mientras, puedes comprar aspirina para mitigar el dolor un poco.
Carmen vuelve a casa con las aspirinas. **(17 verbos)**

En el momento que está tragándose una su marido Roberto entra en la cocina.
-¿Qué te pasa que estás tomando aspirina? Si tienes dolor de muelas, sabes que tienes que hacer, Mañana por la mañana vamos a ver al dentista.
Al día siguiente, Carmen, acompañada por su marido, va a ver al dentista.
Se ha puesto pálida y está temblando cuando entra en la puerta. No tiene que esperar mucho antes de ver al dentista, que le examina la boca con mucho cuidado y paciencia.
-Temo que no pueda empastarte este diente- dice. -Voy a sacarlo, pero es importante que no tengas miedo, No voy a hacerte daño. **(32 verbos)**

Cuando ha terminado Carmen está muy contenta con los resultados. Ahora no tiene dolor de muelas.
-Muchas gracias- dice al salir.
-De nada- contesta el dentista- Pero si no quieres volver pronto, es aconsejable que no comas tantos dulces. **(10 verbos)**

PRACTICE A: Pick out the 75 verbs in this text and use them to complete the verb table below.

VERB	INFINITIVE	ENGLISH	TENSE	PERSON
1.				
2.				
3.				
4.				

Copyright© Vicki Marie Riley 2021. All rights reserved.

BREAK THE LANGUAGE BARRIER LEVEL 4
WWW.ELPRINCIPECENTRE.COM
info@elprincipecentre.com

#				
5.				
6.				
7.				
8.				
9.				
10.				
11.				
12.				
13.				
14.				
15.				
16.				
17.				
18.				
19.				
20.				
21.				
22.				
23.				
24.				
25.				
26.				
27.				
28.				
29.				
30.				
31.				
32.				
33.				
34.				
35.				
36.				
37.				
38.				
39.				
40.				
41.				

Copyright© Vicki Marie Riley 2021. All rights reserved.

BREAK THE LANGUAGE BARRIER LEVEL 4

42.				
43.				
44.				
45.				
46.				
47.				
48.				
49.				
50.				
51.				
52.				
53.				
54.				
55.				
56.				
57.				
58.				
59.				
60.				
61.				
62.				
63.				
64.				
65.				
66.				
67.				
68.				
69.				
70.				
71.				
72.				
73.				
74.				
75.				

PRACTICE B: Translate into English.

Copyright© Vicki Marie Riley 2021. All rights reserved.

BREAK THE LANGUAGE BARRIER LEVEL 4
WWW.ELPRINCIPECENTRE.COM
info@elprincipecentre.com

PRACTICE C: Translate these questions into Spanish and answer in Spanish.

1. Why doesn´t Carmen want to go to the dentist?
2. Why does she speak to her brother, Pepe, in the end?
3. What does Pepe say?
4. Where is the Pharmacy?
5. What does Carmen do while the assistant serves the people?
6. What advice does he give?
7. Who enters the kitchen in the moment that she is swallowing a tablet?
8. What does he say?
9. How is Carmen when she goes in the dentists?
10. Does she have to wait long?
11. Can he fill the tooth?
12. What is he going to do?
13. What is important?
14. How is Carmen when he has finished and why?
15. What is advisable, according to the dentist?
16. Are you scared of the dentist?
17. Why?
18. When was the last time you went to the dentist and what did they do to you?

15. THE IMPERFECT SUBJUNCTIVE.

USES: We should use the imperfect subjunctive in the same cases we would use the present subjunctive, when we are expressing doubt, uncertainty, desire, conjecture etcetera and after certain expressions.

However, as can be imagined, the imperfect would be used when we are talking in the past.

For example:

I hope that it rains today- Espero que **llueva** hoy.
BUT
I was hoping that it would rain yesterday- Esperaba que **lloviera** ayer.

As the main clause of the sentence is in the imperfect, this provokes the use of the imperfect subjunctive rather than the present.

FORMATION:

To form the Imperfect Subjunctive for **ALL** verbs, take the 3rd person plural of the verb in the preterite tense ("they" form), take off the **"ron"** ending, and there you have your base for the imperfect subjunctive.

THIRD PERSON PLURAL PRETERITE	BASE FOR IMPERFECT SUBJUNCTIVE
ESTUDIARON	ESTUDIA
APRENDIERON	APRENDIE
VIVIERON	VIVIE
PUDIERON	PUDIE
SUPIERON	SUPIE
CONDUJERON	CONDUJE
DURMIERON	DURMIE
PUSIERON	PUSIE
FUERON	FUE
VINIERON	VINIE
ANDUVIERON	ANDUVIE

BREAK THE LANGUAGE BARRIER LEVEL 4
WWW.ELPRINCIPECENTRE.COM
info@elprincipecentre.com

ENDINGS:

There are in fact 2 possible sets of endings for this tense (in fact, strictly speaking the subjunctive is a "mood" rather than a tense, but we will refer to it as a tense for ease of understanding). The 2 are outlined below. They can be used interchangeably but the first set are the most common.

a. SET ONE	b. SET TWO
RA	SE
RAS	SES
RA	SE
RAMOS (see note below)	SEMOS (see note below)
RAIS	SEIS
RAN	SEN

NB: The vowel that precedes the first person plural ending ("we"/"nosotros") takes an accent, ie habláramos, comiéramos, viviéramos etc.

PRACTICE A: Find the meanings of these verbs and conjugate them in the Imperfect subjunctive, both forms.

PONER 1.	2.	SER 1.	2.	ESTAR 1.	2.

HACER 1.	2.	ABRIR 1.	2.	SABER 1.	2.

Copyright© Vicki Marie Riley 2021. All rights reserved.

BREAK THE LANGUAGE BARRIER LEVEL 4
WWW.ELPRINCIPECENTRE.COM
info@elprincipecentre.com

TENER 1.	2.	PENSAR 1.	2.	DECIR 1.	2.

PRACTICE B: Translate the following sentences. Use the first form.

1. It was a shame that you couldn´t come to the party.
2. There was no one in the hotel that could help us.
3. He didn´t believe that I wanted to go.
4. They doubted that she was telling the truth.
5. They requested that we had dinner with them.
6. I wanted them to buy the house. She cleaned the house before I arrived.
7. It was probable that you wouldn´t finish.
8. I didn´t think that anyone saw me.
9. It was terrible that they were so ill.
10. I wanted them to speak in Spanish.
11. We hoped that there wouldn´t be a problem.
12. He hoped that you(s) wouldn´t be there.
13. I doubted that it was true.
14. We didn´t want you to know the truth.

16. PRACTICE THE PAST SUBJUNCTIVE- USE THE FIRST FORM.

PRACTICE A: TRANSLATE THESE QUESTIONS INTO SPANISH AND ANSWER THEM IN SPANISH

1. Did you hope that you would live in Spain one day?

2. Did you doubt that Donald Trump would win the election?

3. Was it a shame that Britain came out of Europe?

4. Didn´t you think that it would be so hot in Spain in the summer?

5. Were you looking for a house that had a sea view the last time you came to Spain?

6. Was it important that you should learn the subjunctive?

7. Did you learn to drive as soon as you were old enough?

8. Did you prefer to go on holiday to a country that was warm or cold?

9. Did you used to go to restaurants even if they were expensive?

10. Did you do lots of exercise at the weekends even if it was raining?

11. Did you regret studying Spanish after you encountered the subjunctive?

12. Did you sacrifice a lot so your children could have a good life?

BREAK THE LANGUAGE BARRIER LEVEL 4
WWW.ELPRINCIPECENTRE.COM
info@elprincipecentre.com

17. VIAJE A ESPAÑA

El viaje desde Londres hasta Madrid es muy largo a menos que lo hagas en avión. En tren y barco dura más de treinta y cinco horas. Entonces, cuando llegué en el tren a la Estación del Norte de Madrid estaba muy cansado.

Siempre lo encuentro difícil dormirme en el tren, y desafortunadamente había pasado la noche anterior en un compartimiento de segunda clase con un matrimonio francés que había querido que la ventana quedara abierta. A la vez, unos señores españoles, vestidos de lujo, habían querido que estuviese cerrada. Resultaron muchas discusiones mientras yo intenté dormir sin éxito. (15)

Visitaba España por primera vez, y mis jefes me habían mandado sin aviso previo. Entonces no había tenido tiempo de reservar una habitación en un hotel, ni tenía ninguna dirección que pudiera ayudarme, y empecé a preocuparme. No quería que llegara la noche sin sitio para acostarme, y ya eran las 5 de la tarde. Fue un Domingo en invierno y me sentía un poco perdido y solo en esa ciudad tan grande y desconocida. Pero tenía mi móvil y tarjeta de crédito, y algunos euros en efectivo, así que estaba convencido de que encontrara algo. (18)

PRACTICE A: Pick out the verbs and use them to complete the verb identification table below.

VERB	INFINITIVE	ENGLISH	TENSE	PERSON
1.				
2.				
3.				
4.				
5.				
6.				
7.				
8.				
9.				
10.				
11.				
12.				
13.				
14.				

Copyright© Vicki Marie Riley 2021. All rights reserved.

BREAK THE LANGUAGE BARRIER LEVEL 4
WWW.ELPRINCIPECENTRE.COM
info@elprincipecentre.com

15.				
16.				
17.				
18.				
19.				
20.				
21.				
22.				
23.				
24.				
25.				
26.				
27.				
28.				
29.				
30.				
31.				
32.				
33.				

PRACTICE B: Complete the story. Use at least one form of the imperfect subjunctive.

PRACTICE C: Translate the questions below into Spanish and answer in Spanish.

1. How long does the journey take from London to Madrid by train and boat?
2. How was he feeling when he arrived at Madrid North Station?
3. Why was it difficult to sleep the night before?
4. Why had he had no time to reserve a room?
5. What did he not want?
6. What time was it?
7. What day was it?
8. What season was it?
9. How did he feel?
10. What did he have?
11. What was he convinced of?
12. Have you ever been to Madrid? What was it like?

Copyright© Vicki Marie Riley 2021. All rights reserved.

18. THE PAST SUBJUNCTIVE- "SER" AND "ESTAR"

By now you should most likely know the difference between **"ser"** and **"estar"**!!!
If not, please refer to **"COPPPRINCT"** and **"FLOMMETS"**
(p21)

SER 1.	2.	ESTAR 1.	2.
fuera	fuese	estuviera	estuviese
fueras	fueses	estuvieras	estuvieses
fuera	fuese	estuviera	estuviese
fuéramos	fuésemos	estuviéramos	estuviésemos
fuerais	fueseis	estuvierais	estuvieseis
fueran	fuesen	estuvieran	estuviesen

PRACTICE A: Translate the following sentences using "ser" or "estar". Use the first form.

1. Manuel said that perhaps he would be a doctor one day.
2. We thought that probably they would be there already.
3. Carmen never believed that we would be happy together forever.
4. I doubted that he was really ill.
5. You hoped that I wouldn´t come to the party.
6. When he was young he hoped that he would be married to a nice girl.
7. We wanted to take the blue car but perhaps it was broken.
8. They decided to go to the beach even if they were tired.
9. I tried to arrive at the house as soon as they were ready.
10. Did you(s) buy a house as soon as you(s) were working?
11. I knew that he probably wasn´t a real doctor.
12. María thought it was a shame that they were so nasty.
13. You didn´t believe that anyone was there.
14. We didn´t believe that they were sincere.
15. When Pablo had the accident he thought that he would never be happy again.

BREAK THE LANGUAGE BARRIER LEVEL 4
WWW.ELPRINCIPECENTRE.COM
info@elprincipecentre.com

19. ONE SUNDAY MORNING.

It <u>was</u> 11 o´clock one Sunday morning. There was still very little traffic or people on the streets yet. Antonio and Carmen were walking along the pavement. In front of them their little dog Terri was running and playing. Antonio was carrying the Sunday newspaper and they were chatting and laughing. Suddenly, a car stopped next to them. The driver asked them:

"Excuse me, where is the Town Hall?"

"Go straight on, turn left at the second street, and you will see the Town Hall in front of you. It is a red brick building ..", explained Carmen.

But Antonio disagreed and said:

"That is the Health Centre. The Town Hall is on the same street, at the very end, on the right."

"That´s not true" protested Carmen.
"You are wrong" replied Antonio.
They continued arguing, and their voices got louder and louder and the insults became stronger and stronger. Terri lay down on the pavement tired with all the shouting.

The car started up again and stopped 100 metres further on, at a newspaper kiosk. The driver could still hear Antonio and Carmen arguing, they had not realised that he had gone...

The man in the kiosk gave him the right directions...

PRACTICE A: Pick out the 38 verbs in this story and complete the verb identification table as per the example. Remember that some may be infinitives or gerunds ("ing" words).

	VERB IN CONTEXT	INFINITIVE	SPANISH	TENSE	PERSON
1.	was	To be	ser	preterite	3rd p.pl.
2.					

Copyright© Vicki Marie Riley 2021. All rights reserved.

BREAK THE LANGUAGE BARRIER LEVEL 4
WWW.ELPRINCIPECENTRE.COM
info@elprincipecentre.com

3.				
4.				
5.				
6.				
7.				
8.				
9.				
10.				
11.				
12.				
13.				
14.				
15.				
16.				
17.				
18.				
19.				
20.				
21.				
22.				
23.				
24.				
25.				
26.				
27.				
28.				
29.				
30.				
31.				
32.				
33.				
34.				
35.				
36.				
37.				
38.				

Copyright© Vicki Marie Riley 2021. All rights reserved.

PRACTICE B: Translate the story into Spanish.

PRACTICE C: Translate the questions into Spanish and answer in Spanish.

1. What day was it?
2. What time was it?
3. Was there a lot of traffic on the streets?
4. What were Antonio and Carmen doing?
5. Who was running and playing?
6. What was Antonio carrying?
7. What happened then?
8. What did the driver ask them?
9. What directions did Carmen give him?
10. Why didn´t Antonio agree?
11. What happened to their voices and the insults as they continued arguing?
12. What did Terri do?
13. What did the car do?
14. What could the driver still hear?
15. Who gave him the right directions?

Top Tips!!

6. SOME PHRASES WITH DUAL MEANING WHEN SER/ESTAR USED

estar listo/a- to be ready
ser listo/a- to be clever
estar malo/a- to be ill
ser malo/a- to be bad/ naughty
estar borracho/a- to be drunk
ser un borracho/a- to be an alcoholic
estar despierto- to be awake
ser despierto- to be clever
estar seguro/a- to be certain
ser seguro/a- to be confident

20. VERB TABLES

1. LLEVAR- To

PRESENT	PRESENT PERFECT	PRETERITE

IMPERFECT	PAST PERFECT	FUTURE

CONDITIONAL	PRESENT SUBJUNCTIVE	PAST SUBJUNCTIVE

2. APRENDER - To

PRESENT	PRESENT PERFECT	PRETERITE

IMPERFECT	PAST PERFECT	FUTURE

CONDITIONAL	PRESENT SUBJUNCTIVE	PAST SUBJUNCTIVE

BREAK THE LANGUAGE BARRIER LEVEL 4
WWW.ELPRINCIPECENTRE.COM
info@elprincipecentre.com

3. ESCRIBIR- To

PRESENT	PRESENT PERFECT	PRETERITE

IMPERFECT	PAST PERFECT	FUTURE

CONDITIONAL	PRESENT SUBJUNCTIVE	PAST SUBJUNCTIVE

Copyright© Vicki Marie Riley 2021. All rights reserved.

BREAK THE LANGUAGE BARRIER LEVEL 4
WWW.ELPRINCIPECENTRE.COM
info@elprincipecentre.com

4. PODER- to

PRESENT	PRESENT PERFECT	PRETERITE

IMPERFECT	PAST PERFECT	FUTURE

CONDITIONAL	PRESENT SUBJUNCTIVE	PAST SUBJUNCTIVE

BREAK THE LANGUAGE BARRIER LEVEL 4

5. QUERER- To

PRESENT	PRESENT PERFECT	PRETERITE

IMPERFECT	PAST PERFECT	FUTURE

CONDITIONAL	PRESENT SUBJUNCTIVE	PAST SUBJUNCTIVE

6. PEDIR- To

PRESENT	PRESENT PERFECT	PRETERITE

IMPERFECT	PAST PERFECT	FUTURE

CONDITIONAL	PRESENT SUBJUNCTIVE	PAST SUBJUNCTIVE

BREAK THE LANGUAGE BARRIER LEVEL 4
WWW.ELPRINCIPECENTRE.COM
info@elprincipecentre.com

7. TENER- To

PRESENT	PRESENT PERFECT	PRETERITE

IMPERFECT	PAST PERFECT	FUTURE

CONDITIONAL	PRESENT SUBJUNCTIVE	PAST SUBJUNCTIVE

8. SER- To

PRESENT	PRESENT PERFECT	PRETERITE

IMPERFECT	PAST PERFECT	FUTURE

CONDITIONAL	PRESENT SUBJUNCTIVE	PAST SUBJUNCTIVE

BREAK THE LANGUAGE BARRIER LEVEL 4
WWW.ELPRINCIPECENTRE.COM
info@elprincipecentre.com

9. ESTAR- To

PRESENT	PRESENT PERFECT	PRETERITE

IMPERFECT	PAST PERFECT	FUTURE

CONDITIONAL	PRESENT SUBJUNCTIVE	PAST SUBJUNCTIVE

Copyright© Vicki Marie Riley 2021. All rights reserved.

BREAK THE LANGUAGE BARRIER LEVEL 4

10. PONERSE- To

PRESENT	PRESENT PERFECT	PRETERITE

IMPERFECT	PAST PERFECT	FUTURE

CONDITIONAL	PRESENT SUBJUNCTIVE	PAST SUBJUNCTIVE

BREAK THE LANGUAGE BARRIER LEVEL 4
WWW.ELPRINCIPECENTRE.COM
info@elprincipecentre.com

11. ACOSTARSE- To

PRESENT	PRESENT PERFECT	PRETERITE

IMPERFECT	PAST PERFECT	FUTURE

CONDITIONAL	PRESENT SUBJUNCTIVE	PAST SUBJUNCTIVE

BREAK THE LANGUAGE BARRIER LEVEL 4
WWW.ELPRINCIPECENTRE.COM
info@elprincipecentre.com

12. HACER- To

PRESENT	PRESENT PERFECT	PRETERITE

IMPERFECT	PAST PERFECT	FUTURE

CONDITIONAL	PRESENT SUBJUNCTIVE	PAST SUBJUNCTIVE

Copyright© Vicki Marie Riley 2021. All rights reserved.

BREAK THE LANGUAGE BARRIER LEVEL 4
WWW.ELPRINCIPECENTRE.COM
info@elprincipecentre.com

21. FINISH THE STORY- TERMINA LA HISTORIA

PRACTICE A: Translate The beginning and ending of these stories and fill in the missing part (in Spanish!!)

1. PEDRO ESTABA EN SU COCHE VIAJANDO A TRABAJAR. HABIA MUCHO TRAFICO Y DE REPENTE VI A UN NIÑO DE SOLO UNOS 5 AÑOS CRUZANDO LA CALLE SOLO............

............EL AUTOBUS PARÓ Y PEDRO BAJÓ. NO SABÍA DONDE ESTABA SU COCHE Y SEGURO HABÍA PERDIDO SU TRABAJO PERO ESTABA MUY CONTENTO.

2. ANA Y MARIA TRABAJABAN JUNTAS EN EL BANCO. AQUEL DÍA ENTRARON DOS LADRONES CON PISTOLAS............

.................SE TUMBABAN EN LA PLAYA CON CÓCTELES Y SONRÍAN, QUÉ VIDA MARAVILLOSA!

3. FUE UN DÍA MUY BONITA DE PRIMAVERA Y CARMEN SABÍA QUE IBA A SER UN DÍA BUENO. ESTUVO TOMANDO CAFÉ EN LA COCINA Y DE REPENTE SOÑO SU MOVÍL. CONTESTÓ...FUE ....

............!!DIEZ AÑOS EN EL CARCEL!! NO ERA JUSTO- CARMEN NO COMPRENDÍA QUE HABÍA HECHO PARA MERECER ESTE DESTINO.

BREAK THE LANGUAGE BARRIER LEVEL 4
WWW.ELPRINCIPECENTRE.COM
info@elprincipecentre.com

22. ADJECTIVE PRONOUNS

1. QUALITATIVE -
ENGLISH- "ONE" OR "ONES"
SPANISH- APPROPRIATE DEFINITE ARTICLE PLUS ADJECTIVE.

PRACTICE A:

1. He always bought new cars but I always buy used ones.
2. She prefers short men but I prefer tall ones.
3. They wanted the easy question but we wanted the difficult one.
4. She will think the blonde man is handsome but I will prefer the dark one.
5. The red house would be his and the white one would be hers.
6. Every man wants a luxury car but they always buy the economic ones.
7. I always bought a grey carpet because the white ones always got dirty.
8. Both the dresses are pretty, but you will like the short one more.
9. He has put the big lamps in the living room and the small ones in the bedroom.
10. The big glass is for the red wine and the small one is for the white.

2. QUANTATIVE NUMBERS AS ADJECTIVES (ONE IS THE ONLY ONE TO TAKE A GENDER)

PRACTICE B: Find the Spanish translation:

1. Some
2. Both
3. Each one
4. Too much/too many
5. The rest
6. The two
7. More
8. The majority
9. Less/fewer
10. A lot/ many
11. Nothing
12. None, neither, not anything, not a single one

Copyright© Vicki Marie Riley 2021. All rights reserved.

13. Another, the other
14. Little
15. First
16. Everything/all
17. Last
18. A few
19. Various

PRACTICE C: Use them to translate the following.

1. Some people live in the city and some live in the country
2. I couldn´t decide which brother to marry. I liked them both.
3. I never go shopping with her. It´s dangerous, she buys everything.
4. Carmen loved parties. She was always the last to leave.
5. My husband likes milk so I buy a lot every week.
6. Tomorrow I will buy some Spanish books from the Shopping Centre, would you like one?
7. Last night there were lots of students in the bar. Each one drank a lot.
8. Each girl has had an exam, but several of them haven´t passed.
9. There will be a lot of people at the shops, but few on the beach.
10. We always used to buy a lot of presents at Christmas, but now we don´t buy any.

3. UNSPECIFIED PEOPLE

PRACTICE D: Translate the following:

Someone/ somebody
Anyone/anybody
The one who/he/she who
They who. Those who, the ones who
The oldest
The youngest
No one
Neither one
Everyone, everybody

PRACTICE E: Use them to translate:

1. Often the youngest wore used clothing.
2. Everyone thought it was brilliant.
3. Someone will go with her to the hospital.
4. Nobody is going to tell him the truth.
5. Our favourite customer is she who buys the expensive clothes,
6. There are a lot of differences between the oldest child and the youngest in the family.
7. Oscar Wilde said that a cynic is he who knows the price of everything and the value of nothing.
8. Everyone will suffer from time to time, and the majority will be stronger for the experience.
9. Everyone will be there, but some of them won´t know anybody.
10. Juan and Mateo live in the same apartment, but neither of them has a television.
11. Anyone can wear those trousers.
12. Ramón has given advice to everyone.
13. I will have a party for my birthday. Anyone can come.
14. For these positions, those who will work ten hours a day can request an interview.

4. UNSPECIFIED THINGS

PRACTICE F: Translate the following:

Something/anything
Whichever
The best (thing)
The same (thing)
The worst (thing)
Nothing/not anything

PRACTICE G: Use them to translate:

1. Do you have anything for me?
2. Of all the things in the world, the best is love.
3. It didn´t matter what I wore to his party. He always wore the same thing.

4. Which one do they want? Whichever. It doesn´t matter.
5. It was wonderful when they danced. The best was when they danced the salsa.
6. The service and the atmosphere here are terrible. But the worst is the food.
7. They never brought anything to the party but they ate and drank everything.
8. The worst thing in a relationship would be to not be able to trust the other person.
9. We had thought he was very wise, but in fact he always says the same thing.
10. I don´t know anything about this.
11. Any one of these cars will be good for the winter.
12. These books are interesting. I have been able to read all of them.
13. Any one of these 3 is perfect.

PRACTICE H: Translate

The sign said: "Today is the first day of the rest of your life". If this is true, then what is tomorrow? The second? I can´t believe everything that I read. No one can. Some believe everything. Some people believe the ads in magazines. I suppose that some of them are true but the majority of these ads are lies. They promise everything and deliver nothing.

23. TRANSLATION ENGLISH TO SPANISH- THE GARDENER.

Hugh Grantchester, 26, has been a gardener for four years. He went to Oxford University to study archaeology, but he left after only one term. His father, Hector, is a lawyer, and his mother, Geraldine, is a designer. Hugo tells us about his choice of career. (7)

"When I was 11, we moved to a large house in East Anglia which had a huge garden. We had a gardener who lived in a little cottage at the end of our drive. I used to spend hours watching him work and talking to him. I think I learnt a lot about gardening without realising. One summer, when I was still at school, I had a job at a local garden centre and I knew all the names of the plants, and I could give people advice. (17)

Then I went to University and it was a disaster. I told my parents that I was going to leave and go back to work in the garden centre. They were furious. We had a terrible argument and they didn´t speak to me for months. But I knew it was a waste of time to continue with archaeology and as soon as I started gardening again I knew that I had made the right decision. (16)

I have enjoyed every moment of the last four years and my parents have learned to accept what I do because they can see how happy I am and also because a lot of my university friends have found it difficult to find good jobs. Sometimes people are surprised to learn that their gardener went to University, but I think that it makes them respect my opinion more. I help them plan their gardens and they listen to what I have to say. (19)

Practice A: Pick out the verbs. Identify their equivalent in Spanish, tense, and person and then translate the text into Spanish.

Practice B: Make 10 questions about the text in Spanish and answer them in Spanish.

BREAK THE LANGUAGE BARRIER LEVEL 4
WWW.ELPRINCIPECENTRE.COM
info@elprincipecentre.com

24. TRANSLATION ENGLISH TO SPANISH- THE COOK.

Giles Midmay, 24, has been a professional cook for three years. His father has a big farm in Devon. The family has lived and worked in Devon for over three hundred years. Giles´ younger brother Tobias is studying Farm Management at Exeter University. Giles tells us about his choice of career. (6)

"I think I have always been interested in food. My grandparents lived in a huge old house in Lincolnshire and they had a wonderful cook. She made fantastic traditional English food. I used to love going down to the kitchen and watching her work, and she gave me a lot of tips. I realized that I wanted to be a cook when I was about 12. When other boys chose sport at school I chose cookery. At 15, I had begun to do all the cooking at home for my parent´s dinner parties and had started to make up my own recipes. I knew my parents would not approve of cooking as a career, so I decided to introduce the idea to them slowly. (24)

I told them that I wanted to do a cookery course for fun, and I went to a hotel in Torquay for a month. I enjoyed it so much. I knew I had to tell my parents so one night at dinner I said it. At first, there was silence. Then my father asked me why. I explained that for me cooking was like painting a picture or writing a book. I could see that my father was not happy but he didn´t get angry. He patted me on the shoulder and smiled. My mother kissed me. And now that I have opened my own restaurant, I think that they are very proud of me. However, my grandfather is not so kind, he thinks that I am crazy for giving up farming. (30)

PRACTICE A: PICK OUT THE VERBS. IDENTIFY THEIR EQUIVALENT IN SPANISH, TENSE, AND PERSON AND THEN TRANSLATE INTO SPANISH.
PRACTICE B: TRANSLATE THE QUESTIONS INTO SPANISH AND ANSWER IN SPANISH.

1. How long has Giles´ family lived and worked in Devon?
2. when did he realise that he wanted to be a cook?
3. Why did he decide to introduce the idea slowly to his parents?
4. Where did he go to do a cookery course?
5. What did his parents do when he told them?
6. What does his grandfather think?
7. Do you like cooking?
8. What is the best dish you cook?

Copyright© Vicki Marie Riley 2021. All rights reserved.

BREAK THE LANGUAGE BARRIER LEVEL 4
WWW.ELPRINCIPECENTRE.COM
info@elprincipecentre.com

25. COMMON SPANISH VERBS THAT TAKE A PREPOSITION

1. "a"

Acostumbrarse a- to get used to
Adaptarse a- to adapt oneself to
Animar a- to encourage someone
Aprender a- to learn to do something
Asistir a- to attend something
Ayudar a algien- to help someone
Comenzar a- to start to so something
Contribuir a- to contribute to something
Cuidar a- to look after someone
Dar a- to face
Decidir a- to decide to do something
Empezar a- to start to do something
Enseñar a- to teach someone to do something
Invitar a- to invite to
Ir a- to go to
Negarse a- to refuse to do something
Obligar a- to oblige someone to do something
Ponerse a- to start to do something
Rehusar a- to refuse to do something
Sabor a- to taste of something
Sonar a- to sound like something

2. "con"

aburrirse con- to get bored with
casarse con- to get married to
contar con- to count on
enfadarse con- to get angry with
preocuparse con-to worry about
soñar con- to dream about
tropezar con- to bump into

3. "de"

acabar de- to have just done something
acordarse de- to remember

Copyright© Vicki Marie Riley 2021. All rights reserved.

BREAK THE LANGUAGE BARRIER LEVEL 4
WWW.ELPRINCIPECENTRE.COM
info@elprincipecentre.com

aprovecharse de- to make the most of
arrepentirse de- to regret
cansarse de- to get tired of
dejar de- to stop doing something
depender de- to depend on
encargarse de- to take charge of
hablar de- to talk about
marcharse de- to walk away from (a place)
ocuparse de- to pay attention to
olvidarse de- to forget
parar de- to stop doing something
pensar de- to think of (have an opinion)
quejarse de- to complain
salir de- to leave a place
teminar de- to finish doing something

4. "en"

confiar en- to trust
consentir en- to consent to
consistir en- to consist of
equivocarse en- to make a mistake in something/someone
insistir en- to insist on
mojarse en- to get mixed up in
pensar en- to think about someone/something
quedar en- to agree to something
tardar en- delay in something
trabajar en- to work at something

5. "para"

estar listo/a para- to be ready for
quedarse para- to stay to do something
prepararse para- to prepare oneself for
sentarse para- to sit down to do something
servir para- to be useful for
trabajar para- to work for someone/something, strive to do something

Copyright© Vicki Marie Riley 2021. All rights reserved.

6. "por"

acabar por- to end up doing something
estar por- to be inclined to do something
mirar por- to look after
llorar por- to cry about someone/something
luchar por- to struggle for something
mandar/enviar por- to send by
preocuparse por- to worry about something
trabajar por- to work instead of someone
votar por- to vote for

PRACTICE A: Translate these questions into Spanish and answer in Spanish. They use a mixture of tenses but no subjunctive. Each one uses a verb from the lists of verbs above.

1. Have you got used to living in Spain?
2. What have you done (in order to) adapt yourself to life here?
3. Who can you count on?
4. Have you learned how to ski?
5. When did you start to learn Spanish?
6. Did you get bored with your last job?
7. What do you get angry with?
8. What kind of person would you like to get married to?
9. What do you worry about?
10. Who or what do you dream about?
11. Do you regret leaving the UK?
12. Are you tired of learning Spanish?
13. What do you think about the British Government?
14. Will you forget about Spanish in 10 years?
15. Have you ever agreed to do something that you didn´t want to do?
16. Are you ready for Christmas?
17. What are you working for?
18. Do you want to go to the pub?
19. Who looks after you?
20. Who do you trust?

26. ORDINAL NUMBERS.

1st - PRIMERO/A   2nd - SEGUNDO/A
3rd - TERCERO/A   4th - CUARTO/A
5th - QUINTO   6th - SEXTO/A
7th - SÉPTIMO/A   8th - OCTAVO/A
9th - NOVENO/A   10th - DÉCIMO/A

PRACTICE A: TRANSLATE.

1. I lived in the second house on the left and Miguel lived in the sixth.
2. I don´t know who lives in the eighth house but Carmen lives in the seventh.
3. My car is the third on the right and Pedro´s car is the fourth.
4. The Bible tells us that Adam was the first person and Eve was the second.
5. For me, the first film in a series will always be better than the second.
6. Tom Cruise´s third film was better than his fourth.
7. Lee Child´s fifth book was more exciting than the sixth, but his seventh was the best of all.
8. The first day of the week is Monday and the seventh is Sunday.
9. August is the eighth month, September the ninth, and October is the tenth.
10. The first time I went to Spain was better than the second, the third was a lot of fun but the fourth was my favourite.

PRACTICE B: TRANSLATE.

When we used to go out, my best friend and I competed to see who could drink the most vodka. For example, I would drink one and he would drink two. Then I would drink three and he would drink four. The first person to stop drinking was the loser and the other person won. The first was easy. And the second was too. The third was also good. From the fourth it became more difficult. The fifth was a challenge, also the sixth, the seventh and the eighth. The ninth was always a blur and I never remembered the tenth!!

27. CONVERSATION PRACTICE-

PRACTICE A- Make this conversation in Spanish.

At the Doctors

Doctor- Say good morning, ask what the problem is.
Patient- Explain that you have been having problems sleeping, and you have a slight headache most of the time. You have no energy, and you don´t ever want to do anything.
Doctor- Ask how long they have felt like this.
Patient- Tell them how long.
Doctor-Ask if they are taking any medication, have there been changes in their lifestyle, are they worried about anything, do they have a headache in this moment etc etc Do they drink enough liquids, take exercise and eat healthily?
Patient- Answer all the questions and tell the Doctor that the headache is worse in the evening and after you have been on the computer. Ask him if he thinks it is anything serious.

Doctor and Patient- continue the dialogue, and come to an agreement about a diagnosis. Could be high blood pressure, dehydration, depression or need glasses etc etc Make suggestions and eliminate possibilities. Take blood pressure etc

Doctor-Tell them you need to send them for a blood test. Explain how to make the appointment etc and tell them to come back in 2 weeks.
Patient-Ask if you can have breakfast before the test.
Doctor- Explain that they have to come at 8.00 a.m and not eat or drink beforehand.

Doctor and Patient- Say your goodbyes

28. LA GENERATION "DINK"

PRACTICE A: Translate into English

Hace algunos años era común la imagen de la clásica pareja rodeada, por lo menos, de dos niños. Las parejas tenían que "apretarse el cinturón" para que el dinero alcanzara y así cubrir todos los gastos que un hogar representa. No obstante, la realidad actual muestra un panorama diferente de la sociedad. Las parejas modernas tienen otras preocupaciones entre las cuales los hijos no son un tema relevante. A estas parejas se les conoce como "DINKS" (double income, no kids, o en español- "doble sueldo, no niños").

Estas parejas (adultos entre los 25 y 39 años) se mantienen ocupadas planeando sus próximas vacaciones (viajan con mucha frecuencia). Se mantienen al día sobre los últimos avances tecnológicos, visitan tiendas lujosas, cenan en los restaurantes más caros y de "última moda". También por supuesto mantienen una apariencia física impecable, su imagen es un reflejo de éxito y vanguardia.

Sin embargo, en países conservadores como México, Guatemala o Bolivia este concepto no es muy popular entre las generaciones pasadas. A los "DINKS" siempre se les cuestiona -¿cuándo vais a tener hijos? ¿no quieren formar un hogar? O se les recrimina con la idea "un matrimonio feliz es un matrimonio con hijos". Por su parte, estas parejas viven felices al valorar todo lo que pueden lograr cuando invierten su sueldo en bienes que no podrían alcanzar si fueran padres.

Para muchas personas este modo de vida del NO HIJOS es egoísta. Para otras es una nueva manera de experimentar la libertad en todos los ámbitos. Es un hecho que la generación DINK se impone a los papeles tradicionales de las relaciones de pareja y nos hace pensar en el rumbo que tomará la nueva sociedad del siglo XXI.

Y tú, ¿eres un DINK?

29. POSTSCRIPT

There it is.
The weird and wonderful subjunctive is a mystery and an enigma to the best of us, so please don't expect to take it all in the first time you look at it.
Repetition and practice is essential for fluidity and confidence with your Spanish, but remember not to be too hard on yourself and expect immediate perfection. You will get it wrong many times before you get it right!!

When you are confident with all the components of this Level 4 course you should be communicating effectively in Spanish in the past tenses and ready to move on to Level 5.

Don´t forget the YouTube channel, where you will find the audio of all the exercises. The link is below, the videos are numbered and the page numbers are in the description. Please give a thumbs up if you find the video useful, and subcribe for updates (this is FREE, no cost involved).
You will also find all social media links and contact details below.

Lastly, if you have the time and feel so inclined, please leave a review on Amazon of this book and how it has helped you to learn Spanish. Thank you 😊

Happy practising!!!
Vicki

Facebook: https://www.facebook.com/elprincipecentre/
Instagram: https://www.instagram.com/elprincipecentre/
Twitter: @PrincipeCentre
YouTube: https://www.youtube.com/channel/UCm38MRBMVXrV6JblhmQ7xOg
Blog: Confessions of a Spanish teacher: https://confessionsofaspanishteacher.wordpress.com/

Thank you all for your continuing support

Keep practicing and more importantly stay safe and healthy.

BREAK THE LANGUAGE BARRIER LEVEL 4
WWW.ELPRINCIPECENTRE.COM
info@elprincipecentre.com

30. KEY TO "TOP TIPS"

There are not so many "Top Tips" in this Level for the simple reason that most tips for learning Spanish are already in Levels 1, 2 and 3!!

However, I hope you find these useful:

	Page number
1. VERBS THAT CHANGE MEANING IN THE PRETERITE	7
2. SOME FALSE FRIENDS THAT DON'T MEAN WHAT YOU THINK	10
3. VERBS MY STUDENTS OFTEN CONFUSE	13
4. COMMON MISTAKES ALL MY STUDENTS MAKE	18
5. SLANG EXPRESSIONS TO MAKE YOU SOUND LIKE A SPANIARD	25
6. PHRASES WITH DUAL MEANINGS SER VERSUS ESTAR	42

Copyright© Vicki Marie Riley 2021. All rights reserved.

31. ANSWER KEY

1. INTRODUCE YOURSELF.

DINOS ALGO SOBRE TÍ...

1. ¿Dónde trabajabas/ trabajaste antes?
2. ¿Pór que y cuándo viniste a España?
3. ¿Tienes niños?
4. ¿Cómo es tu pareja?
5. ¿Irás de vacaciones el año que viene?
6. ¿Vivirías en otro país?
7. ¿Cómo has practicado el español desde tu última clase?
8. ¿Cómo vas a practicar después de este libro?
9. ¿Cuánto tiempo has estudiado español?
10. ¿Qué hiciste el fin de semana pasado?
11. ¿Hablarías con un desconocido en un tren?
12. ¿Qué son los problemas más grandes que has tenido en aprender español?
13. ¿Qué quieres lograr después de este libro?
14. ¿Cuándo fue la última vez que hablaste español?
15. ¿Has comprado un coche nuevo este año?
16. ¿Cuántos idiomas hablas?
17. ¿Cuándo es tu cumpleaños?
18. ¿Qué hiciste en tu cumpleaños el año pasado?
19. ¿Dónde vivías cuando eras niño?
20. ¿Estarías felíz viviendo en otro país?

FREE ANSWERS

BREAK THE LANGUAGE BARRIER LEVEL 4
WWW.ELPRINCIPECENTRE.COM
info@elprincipecentre.com

2. TRANSLATION AND COMPREHENSION PRACTICE WITH VARIOUS TENSES, ENGLISH TO SPANISH- ME HABÍAN ROBADO.

PRACTICE A:

VERB	INFINITIVE	SPANISH	TENSE	PERSON
1. I was walking	To walk	andar	imperfecto	1st sing
2. pushed	To push	empujar	preterite	3rd p.sing
3. I found myself	To to find	encontrar	preterite	1st p.sing
4. realising	To realise	Darse cuenta	infinitive	
5. was	To be	estar	preterite	1st p.sing
6. I started	To start	empezar	preterite	1st p.sing
7. to shout	To shout	gritar	infinitive	
8. I realised	To realise	Dares cuenta	preterite	1st p.sing
9. I hadn´t hurt myself	To hurt oneself	Hacerse daño	past perfect	1st p.sing
10. I put (in)	To put in	meter	preterite	1st p.sing
11. discovered	To discover	descubrir	preterite	1st p.sing
12. I had been robbed	To rob	robar	past perfect	3rd p.plural
13. approached	To approach	acercarse	preterite	3rd p.plural
14. to ask	To ask	preguntar	infinitive	
15. needed	To need	necesitar	preterite	1st p.sing
16. I said	To say	decir	preterite	1st p.sing
17. had been stolen	To steal	robar	past perfect	3rd p. plural
18. said	To say	decir	preterite	3rd p.sing
19. he had seen	To see	ver	past perfect	3rd p.sing
20. run	To run	correr	infinitive	
21. it was	To be	ser	preterite	3rd p.sing
22. he had said	To say	decir	past perfect	3rd p.sing
23. he began	To begin	empezar	preterite	3rd p.sing
24. to run	To run	correr	infinitive	
25. he returned	To return	volver	preterite	3rd p.sing
26. saying	To say	decir	gerund	
27. he had seen	To see	ver	past perfect	3rd p.sing
28. they had followed	To follow	seguir	past perfect	3rd p.plural
29. he had disappeared	To disappear	disaparecer	past perfect	3rd p. sing
30. I wanted	To want	querer	imperfect	1st p.sing

Copyright© Vicki Marie Riley 2021. All rights reserved.

BREAK THE LANGUAGE BARRIER LEVEL 4
WWW.ELPRINCIPECENTRE.COM
info@elprincipecentre.com

31. to thank	To thank	Dar las gracias	infinitive	
32. we went	To go	ir	preterite	1st p.plural
33. I bought	To buy	comprar	preterite	1st p.sing
34. I was carrying	To carry	llevar	imperfecto	1st p.sing
35. I went	To go	ir	preterite	1st p.sing
36. to make	To make	hacer	infinitive	
37. I had been robbed	To rob	robar	past perfect	1st p.sing
38. wasn´t	To be	ser	imperfecto	3rd p.sing
39. I was also carrying	To carry	llevar	imperfecto	1st p.sing

PRACTICE B:

El otro día yo caminaba por la calle cuando de repente alguien me empujó y me encontré en el suelo sin darme cuenta. Primero estuve tan asustado que empezé a gritar como un idiota. Entonces me di cuenta que no me había hecho daño, pero cuando meté la mano en el bolsillo de los pantalones descubrí que me habían robado. Muchas personas me acercaron para preguntarme si necesitle ayuda.
Dije que me habían robado de cartero y un chico dijo que había visto a alguien correr por la calle y sin duda fue el ladrón. Tan pronto como había dicho esto, él empezó a correr en esa dirección. Después de un rato volvió diciendo que había visto el ladrón y que le había seguido un buen rato, pero que de repente había disaparecido en un calejón.
Quería darle las gracias, entonces fuimos a un bar y le compré una bebida con los pocos euros que tenía sueltos en mi bolsillo. Entonces fui a la Comisaria para hacer una denuncia que me habían robado. En mi cartero, ádemas del dinero, que no fue mucho, llevaba también mi tarjeta de identidad, mi carnet de conducir y mis tarjetas de crédito

PRACTICE C:

El otro día él caminaba por la calle cuando de repente alguien le empujó y se encontró en el suelo sin darse cuenta. Primero estuvo tan asustado que empezó a gritar como un idiota. Entonces se dio cuenta que no se había hecho daño, pero cuando metó la mano en el bolsillo de los pantalones descubrió que le habían robado. Muchas personas le acercaron para preguntarle si necesitó ayuda.
Dije que le habían robado de cartero y un chico dijo que había visto a alguien correr por la calle y sin duda fue el ladrón. Tan pronto como había dicho esto, él empezó a correr en esa dirección. Después de un rato volvió diciendo que había

visto el ladrón y que le había seguido un buen rato, pero que de repente había disaparecido en un callejón.

Él quería darle las gracias, entonces fueron a un bar y le compró una bebida con los pocos euros que tenía sueltos en su bolsillo. Entonces fue a la Comisaria para hacer una denuncia que le habían robado. En su cartero, ádemas del dinero, que no fue mucho, llevaba también su tarjeta de identidad, su carnet de conducir y sus tarjetas de crédito

PRACTICE D:. FREE ANSWERS. If you want me to check them please send to info@elprincipecentre.com.

3. THE PRESENT SUBJUNCTIVE 1- FORMATION AND EXPRESSIONS OF DESIRE.

PRACTICE A:

A. To hope, expect.
B. To demand
C. To insist on
D. God willing
E. To request
F. To prefer
G. To want
H. To requested
I. To suggest

1. I would prefer that you(s) take the bus.
2. They insist that I have the house.
3. You want them to love you a lot.
4. I hope that they can dance well
5. He/she requests you sit down now.
6. They hope that she will live in that house

PRACTICE B:

1. Espero que me llame mañana.
2. Quiere que comas el bocadillo.
3. Quieren que escribamos una carta.
4. Esperamos que estés bien.

BREAK THE LANGUAGE BARRIER LEVEL 4
WWW.ELPRINCIPECENTRE.COM
info@elprincipecentre.com

5. Quiere que lo hagamos.
6. Insisto en que lo hagan.
7. Sugerimos que lo pruebas,
8. Siempre insisten que trabaje yo con ellos.
9. Ruega que lleguemos a las 9.
10. Prefieren que salgamos el viernes.
11, Espero que les conozcas,
12. Insistimos en que comas con nosotros.
13. ¿Quieres que cuente yo el dinero?
14, Sugiero que salgamos todos ahora,
15, Sugieren que ingresemos el dinero en el banco,

PRACTICE C: TRANSLATION

Mañana es el primer día de la vida nueva de mi hija, Espero que todo le vaya bien. Mi nuevo yerno parece muy simpático, pero prefiero que sea más sincero que amable. Quiero que siempre le muestres amor y respeto, Quiero que me diga directamente como mejorará la vida de mi hija. Voy a pedir que siempre le diga la verdad. Si sugiere que no la ayude con los niños estaré muy triste,

4. THE PRESENT SUBJUNCTIVE 2- DOUBT OR IGNORANCE.

PRACTICE A:

1, I doubt they will come.
2, They fear it is too late,
3, It doesn´t seem they are here,
4, Dont imagine that they have good intentions.
5. We dont think that we will go to England in June.
6. I dont think that he wants to go.

PRACTICE B:

1. Dudamos que trabajen en esa factoria.
2. No supongo que me digan la verdad.
3. No cree que esté felíz.
4. No estoy seguro de que vayan.
5. No piensan que la comida esté listo.

Copyright© Vicki Marie Riley 2021. All rights reserved.

BREAK THE LANGUAGE BARRIER LEVEL 4
WWW.ELPRINCIPECENTRE.COM
info@elprincipecentre.com

6. No estamos convencidos de que nos conozcais.
7. ¿Por que no cree que seas sincero?
8, Duda que sepamos la respuesta.
9. No están seguros de que lleguemos a la hora.
10, ¿Por qué no estás convencido de que funcione bien?
11. No parece que quiera ir.
12. No estamos seguros de que pueda hacer esto.
13. Ella no cree que estemos juntos.

PRACTICE C: TRANSLATION

Dudo que David sepa que planeo una sorpresa para él. No parece posible que tenga casi 50, y no me imagino que lo crea él tampoco. No supongo que espere una fiesta y dudo que le guste toda la atención, No estoy convencida de que esté felíz. Sin embargo, no supongo que diga nada. Sólo quiero que todo le vaya bien.

5. THE PRESENT SUBJUNCTIVE 3- IMPERSONAL OPINION.

PRACTICE A:

1. It.s a shame that I cant go.
2. Its ridiculous that they cant do it.
3. Its terrible that he doesnt have work.
4. Its neccesary that you learn the subjunctive in order to speak Spanish well.
5. Hopefully we wont wake up late.

PRACTICE B:

1. Es mejor que no bebamos alcohol.
2. Conviene que cierres las ventanas.
3. Es preferible que no comas carne.
4. Es improbable que quiera ir.
5. Es necesario que lleves una traductora contigo.
6. Es imprtante que nadie sepa la verdad.
7. Puede ser que viven en otra ciudad ahora.
8. Es ridiculo que tantos niños no sepan deletrear.
9. Es imposible que terminemos el trabajo esta semana.
10. Es increíble que hable tantos idiomas.

Copyright© Vicki Marie Riley 2021. All rights reserved.

11. Es una lástima que el vino sea tan caro en Inglaterra.
12. Es fantástico que tenga tantos amigos.
13. Puede ser que David sea alto y guapo.
14. Es imposible que nos quedemos en Inglaterra todo el verano.
15. Ojalá que tengan más tiempo.

PRACTICE C: TRANSLATION

Anoche fui al cine por primera vez. Es posible que sea la única persona que nunca ha ido. Hay tantas razones tontas. Por ejemplo, es ridículo que estè tan nerviosa de sitios públicos. Es mejor que una persona tenga la libertad de salir a cualquier momento si eso es lo que él o ella necesita hacer. También, es increíble que tngamos que sentarnos al lado de desconocidos en el cine, eso es muy difícil para mí- Es mejor que nos sentemos aparte de otras personas pero sé que esto es imposible. Ojalá que no tenga todas esta fobias.

6. THE PRESENT SUBJUNCTIVE 4 - UNCOMPLETED ACTION.

PRACTICE A:

1. Unless
2. Before
3. As long as
4. When
5. After
6. In case of
7. Until
8. While
9. In order that
10. Without
11. As soon as

PRACTICE B:

1. I will call you as soon as I arrive.
2. We wont be going unless you do.
3. I study a lot at home in case there is an exam.
4. I work so that we can eat.

5. He/she will play the piano as long as you(s) sing.
6. I will live here until I have another house.
7. We are studying the subjunctive in order that we can understand better.
8. José prepares the salad while I make the paella.
9. I wont eat the paella unless you eat it too.
10. When you(s) can, bring me the papers.
11. We are going home after they bring us the bill.

PRACTICE C:

1. No comeré hasta que tenga hambre.
2. Te he escrito una nota para que te acuerdes comprar leche.
3. Te sentirás mejor después de que tomes esta medicina.
4. No se casará con ninguna mujer al menos que sea rica.
5. Secaré los platos mientras los laves.
6. Lo creeré cuando lo vea.
7. Le llamaremos de nuevo en caso de que se olvide.
8. No compraran nada al menos de que sea barato.
9. Cada día toma una pastilla para que no se enferme.
10. Debes cepillarte los dientes antes de que vayamos al dentista.
11. No podéis ayudarle hasta que cambie su vida.
12. ¿Puedes hacer estos deberes cuando tengas tiempo?
13. No van al médico sin que hagan una cita primero.
14. Cerrará la puerta después de que entre en la habitación.
15. Hablaremos much español tan pronto como entendamos el subjunctivo.

PRACTICE D: TRANSLATION

David promete que me llamará tan pronto que llegue alli. Sin embargo, problamente sólo llamará cuando no esté ocupado con el trabajo. Pienso que me dirá todo cuando llegue a casa. No llamará al menos que pase un milagro. Me puede llamar mientras que esté en el tren, pero no hará eso en caso de que pierde algo interesante. Llamará con tal que le llame yo a menudo y le digo que quiero que vuelva. Estaremos felices despues de que termine el trabajo

7. THE PRESENT SUBJUNCTIVE 5- INDEFINITE OBJECT.

PRACTICE A:

BREAK THE LANGUAGE BARRIER LEVEL 4
WWW.ELPRINCIPECENTRE.COM
info@elprincipecentre.com

1. We prefer a country that has a lot of life.
2. They are looking for a dog that doesnt bark much.
3. He/she needs a flat that has a lift.
4. There is nobody at home that has the key.
5. We want a restaurant that sells tapas.
6. I am looking for a hairdresser that knows how to cut hair well.
7. She wants a husband that is rich.
8. There must be someone here that I know,
9. For my birthday I want a ring with an enormous diamond.
10. We all want a child that is happy.

BREAK THE LANGUAGE BARRIER LEVEL 4
WWW.ELPRINCIPECENTRE.COM
info@elprincipecentre.com

PRACTICE B:

1. Buscamos una secretaria que sea eficiente.
2. Quieren un trabajo que pague mucho dinero.
3. Hay algunas tiendas por aqui que vendan sellos?
4. Necesitas un coche que no cueste mucho.
5. ¿Hay alguien aqui que hable Español?
6. Carlos busca una escuela que enseñe francés.
7. Quiero una falda que sea roja.
8. No hay nadie aqui que te pueda ayudar.
9. Para mi cumpeañosquiero un movíl que tome fotos.
10. Quiero vivir en un mundo donde no haya pobreza.
11. ¿Hay alguien aqui que tenga boli?
12. Necesitan a alguien que trabaje mucho.
13. Busca un sofá que tenga tres asientos.
14. Necesitan un amigo que viva cercano.
15. Queremos una habitación de hotel que tenga buena vista.

PRACTICE C: TRANSLATION

Fui de vacaciones con mi amiga el mes pasado. Nunca iré con ella más. Quiere demasiado. Primero, quiere un hotel que esté muy cerca de la playa. Después, quiere una habitación que esté en la plata baja pero que tenga vista al mar. También quiere que este hotel cueste menos de doscianto euros por una semana. Quiere comidas que sean ricas y cocteles que tengan mucho alcohol. Le dije que no hay ningun hotel en España que proprcione todas estas cosas por doscientos euros. De hecho, dije que no hay nadie en el mundo que comprenda sus demandas.

8. THE PRESENT SUBJUNCTIVE 6- "QUIZÁ" AND "AUNQUE".

PRACTICE A:

1. Quizá tenga el dinero.
2. Aunque se vaya Carlos, no me quedaré.
3. Aunque quieran ver la tele, no pueden.
4. Aunque pienses que eres feo, todo el mundo sabe que eres guapo.

5. Aunque les grites, no cambiarán.
6. Quizá seamos tontos.
7. Quizá podamos ir.
8. Aunque sepa yo la verdad, no te la diré.
9. Aunque corres, no cogerás el autobús.
10. Quizá compren la casa hoy.
11. Aunque esté enfermo, tiene que trabajar.
12. Quizá vivamos en los Estados Unidos un día.
13. Aunque quieras ir, no puedes.
14. Aunque puedan llamar, no quiero hablar con ellos.
15. Aunque diga yo que sí, ya es demasiado tarde.

PRACTICE B: TRANSLATION

No hay nadie que sea tan buena compañia como mi novio David. Es genial que venga a España este fin de semana como no le he visto durante dos semanas. Espero que haga su famoso cóctel de gambas otra vez, pero dudo que lo haga este fin de semana porque lo hizo la última vez. Aunque no prepare este plato, prepará algo rico. Quizá le pida, para que compre las gambas especiales cuando llegue. Espero que diga que sí.

10. THE PRESENT SUNBJUNCTIVE- "SER" AND "ESTAR".

PRACTICE A:

1. Espero que no esté enfermo.
   Espero que sea guapo.

2. Ojalá nuestro vecinos sean españoles.
   Ojalá nuestros vecinos no estén en la casa.

3. ¿Quieres que sea enfermera?
   ¿Quieres que esté alli contigo.

4. No creo que esté contenta.
   No creo que sea alta.

5. No parece que sea fiesta muy buena.

BREAK THE LANGUAGE BARRIER LEVEL 4
WWW.ELPRINCIPECENTRE.COM
info@elprincipecentre.com

    No parece que esté abierto.

6. Dudamos que sean muy agradables.
   Dudamos que los bancos estén abiertos a esta hora.

7. No puedo ir hasta que esté abierto.
   No puedo ir hasta que sea invierno.

8. Tan pronto como sean noche iré.
   Tan pronto como esté abierto iré.

9. Quizá sean altos, morenos y guapos.
   Quizá estén en el bar.

10. Aunque sea enferma, no me gusta.
    Aunque esté enferma, no tengo tiempo para ella.

11. Es imposible que sean amigos.
    Es imposible que estén en el país.

12. Es necesario que que seamos siempre educados.
    Es necesario que siempre estemos alli con ellos.

13. Cuando seas médico, te llamaré.
    Cuando estés en España, me llamarás.

14. Quizá yo sea cantante un día.
    Quizá esté cansado el viernes después del trabajo.

11. PRACTICE THE PRESENT SUBJUNCTIVE.

PRACTICE A:

FREE ANSWERS.

PRACTICE B:

1. Mis amigos dicen que este año no nevaré.

Copyright© Vicki Marie Riley 2021. All rights reserved.

BREAK THE LANGUAGE BARRIER LEVEL 4
WWW.ELPRINCIPECENTRE.COM
info@elprincipecentre.com

2. El médico no considera que el paciente ande bien.
3. Es posible que necesitemos más horas para estudiar.
4. ¿Piensas que es posible que que haga veinte grados en Murcia en diciembre?
5. Todas las teorias juntas no son capaces de explicar esto.
6. Las calles no son anchas, pero quizá sea porque no hay espacio.
7. Es bueno que todos comuniquemos bien.
8. ¿Por qué o por qué tenemos que aprender el subjunctivo?
9. Quiero una recepcionista que hable bien el inglés.
10. La recepcionista en el médico habke 5 idiomas distintos.
11. Dice que es buena persona.
12. No creemos que sea muy buena persona.

12. CONVERSATION PRACTICE PRESENT SUNJUNCTIVE.

1. ¿Harías una barbacoa el fin de semana aunque llueva?
2. ¿Te importa que tus amigos sean sinceros?
3. ¿No piensas que España sea mejor de tu país?
4. ¿Quitas el edredón de tu cama en cuanto que llegue el verano?
5. ¿Dudas que haga calor este verano en España?
6. ¿Se van normalmente los problemas aunque no hagas nada?
7. ¿Es imposible que aprendas el subjunctivo?
8. ¿No parece que el tiempo haga bien el domingo, todavía planeas salir?
9. ¿Te gustaría tener una casa que tenga más dormitorios que la tuya?
10. ¿Te gustaría comprar un coche que vaya muy rápido?
11. ¿Qué clases de español harás cuándo aprendes el subjunctivo?
12. ¿Prefieres un restaurante que venda tapas?
13. ¿Hay escuela en tu barrio que haga clases de español?
14. ¿Irías en un crucero aunque sea muy caro?
15. ¿Es probable que compres un coche nuevo dentro de poco?
16. ¿Tendrías un perro que ladre mucho?
17. ¿Qué harás en cuanto que te jubiles?
18. ¿Tienes una tienda en to barrio que venda comida china?
19. ¿ Qué esperas que logres en tu curso de español?
20. ¿Qué prefieres, un coche que sea rápido y deportivo o un coche que sea fiable?

Copyright© Vicki Marie Riley 2021. All rights reserved.

BREAK THE LANGUAGE BARRIER LEVEL 4
WWW.ELPRINCIPECENTRE.COM
info@elprincipecentre.com

13. PRESENT SUBJUNCTIVE IN CONTEXT

PRACTICE A:

VERB	INFINITIVE	SPANISH	TENSE	PERSON
1. are you	To be	estar	present	2 p. sing
2. I hope	To hope	esperar	present	1 p. sing
3. you are	To be	estar	subjunctive	2 p. plural
4. I wish	To wish	desear	present	1 p. sing
5. brings	To bring	traer	subjunctive	3 p. sing
6. you see	To see	ver	subjunctive	2 p. plural
7. I hope	To hope	esperar	present	1 p. sing
8. you forgive	To forgive	perdonar	subjunctive	2 p. sing
9. I have had	To have	tener	past perfect	1 p. sing

10. to write	To write	escribir	infinitive	
11. writing	To write	escribir	infinitive	
12. is	To be	ser	present	3 p.sing
13. reserve	To reserve	reservar	subjunctive	2 p. sing
14. is	To be	estar	subjunctive	3 p.sing
15. doesn´t matter	To matter	importar	present	3 p.sing
16. is	To be	ser	subjunctive	3 p.sing
17. is	To be	ser	subjunctive	3 p.sing
18. will have to	To have to	Tener que	future	1 p. sing
19. spend	To spend	pasar	infinitive	
20. wants	To want	querer	present	3. p. sing
21. to make	To make	hacer	subjunctive	1 p. sing
22. opening	To open	abrir	infinitive	
23. you want	To want	querer	present	2 p.sing
24. to tell	To tell	decir	subjunctive	1 p.sing
25. I wasn´t	To be	estar	imperfect	1 p. sing
26. having to	To have to	Tener que	infinitive	
27. be	To be	estar	infinitive	
28. I am	To be	estar	present	1 p. sing
29. it will be	To be	ser	subjunctive	2 p. sing

Copyright© Vicki Marie Riley 2021. All rights reserved.

30. It is	To be	ser	present	I p. sing
31. to see each other	To see each other	verse	infinitive	
32. it will be	To be	ser	subjunctive	3 p. sing

PRACTICE B:

Querido Richard,

¿Cómo estás? Espero que todos estéis bien y deseo que el Año Nuevo os traiga todo tipa de buenas cosas y que veais todos vuestros sueños realizados. Espero que perdones mi largo silencio pero casi no he tenido tiempo para escribirte. La razón para escribirte es que me reserves, del 21 de enoero, una habitación individual en un buen hotel que esté cerca del centro de la ciudad. No importa que sea cara.

El más probable es que tenga que pasar un par de meses en tu país, como mi empresa quiere que hago unestudio de la posibilidad de abrir una rama alli. Si quieres que te diga la verdad, al principio no estaba contenta con la idea de tener que estar fuera de casa por mucho tiempo, pero ahora estoy felíz que será así, Será buena oportunidad para vernos otra vez y quizá sea una experiencia buena para mi futuro profesional.

Tengo ganas de verte pronto

Abrazos

María

PRACTICE C: FREE ANSWER

14. DOLOR DE MUELAS

PRACTICE A:

VERB	INFINITIVE	ENGLISH	TENSE	PERSON
1. tiene	tener	To have	present	3 p. sing
2. quiere	querer	To want	present	3 p. sing
3. sepa	saber	To know	subjunctive	3 p. sing

BREAK THE LANGUAGE BARRIER LEVEL 4
WWW.ELPRINCIPECENTRE.COM
info@elprincipecentre.com

4. quiere	querer	To want	present	3 p. sing
5. ir	ir	To go	infinitive	
6. ver	ver	To see	infinitive	
7. tiene	tener	To have	present	3 p. sing
8. sea	ser	To be	subjunctive	3 p. sing
9. puede	poder	To be able	present	3 p. sing
10. aguantar	aguantar	To stand	infinitive	
11. habla	hablar	To speak	present	3 p. sing
12. dice	decir	To say/ tell	present	3 p. sing
13. puede	poder	To be able	present	3 p. sing
14. ser	ser	To be	infinitive	
15. tenga	tener	To have	subjunctive	3 p. sing
16. aliviar	aliviar	To relieve	infinitive	
17. va	ir	To go	present	3 p. sing
18. está	estar	To be	present	3 p. sing
19. sirve	servir	To serve	present	3 p. sing
20. mira	mirar	To look at	present	3 p. sing
21. buscando	buscar	To look for	gerund	
22. encuentra	encontrar	To find	present	3 p. sing
23. explica	explicar	To explain	present	3 p. sing
24. pide	pedir	To ask	present	3 p. sing
25. se sonrie	sonreirse	To smile	present	3 p. sing
26. puedo	poder	To be able	present	1 p. sing
27. ayudar	ayudar	To help	infinitive	
28. conviene	convenir		present	3 p. sing
29. vayas	ir	To be	subjunctive	2 p. sing
30. puedes	poder	To be able	present	2 p. sing
31. comprar	comprar	To buy	infinitive	
32. mitigar	mitigar	To mitigate	infinitive	
33. vuelve	volver	To return	present	3 p. sing
34. está	estar	To be	present	3 p. sing
35. tragándose	tragarse	To swallow	gerund	
36. entra	entrar	To enter	present	3 p. sing
37. pasa	pasar	To pass/happen	present	3 p. sing
38. estás	estar	To be	present	2 p. sing
39. tomando	tomar	To take	gerund	
40. tienes	tener	To have	present	2 p. sing

Copyright© Vicki Marie Riley 2021. All rights reserved.

BREAK THE LANGUAGE BARRIER LEVEL 4
WWW.ELPRINCIPECENTRE.COM
info@elprincipecentre.com

41. sabes	saber	To know	present	2 p. sing
42. tienes que	Tener que	To have to	present	2 p. sing
43. hacer	hacer	To do/make	infinitive	
44. vamos	ir	To go	present	1 p. plural
45. ver	ver	To see	infinitive	
46. va	ir	To go	present	3 p. sing
47. ver	ver	To see	infinitive	
48. se ha puesto	ponerse	To turn	Present perfect	3 p. sing
49. está	estar	To be	present	3 p. sing
50. temblando	temblar	To tremble	gerund	
51. entra	entrar	To enter	present	3 p. sing
52. tiene que	Tener que	To have to	present	3 p. sing
53. esperar	esperar	To wait	infinitive	
54. ver	ver	To see	infinitive	
55. examina	examinar	To examine	present	3 p. sing
56. temo que	Temer que	To be afraid	present	1 p. sing
57. pueda	poder	To be able	subjunctive	3 p. sing
58. empastar	empastar	To fill	infinitive	
59. dice	decir	To say	present	3 p. sing
60. voy	ir	To go	present	1 p. sing
61. sacar	sacar	To take out	infinitive	
62. es	ser	To be	present	3 p. sing
63. tengas	tener	To have	subjunctive	2 p. sing
64. voy	ir	To go	present	1 p. sing
65. hacer	hacer	To do/make	infinitive	
66. ha terminado	terminar	To finish	Present perfect	3 p. sing
67. está	estar	To be	present	3 p. sing
68. tiene	tener	To have	present	3 p. sing
69. dice	decir	To say/tell	present	3 p. sing
70. salir	salir	To leave/go out	infinitive	
71. contesta	contestar	To answer	present	3 p. sing
72. quieres	querer	To want	present	2 p. sing
73. volver	volver	To return	infinitive	
74. es	ser	To be	present	3 p. sing
75. comas	comer	To eat	subjunctive	2 p. sing

Copyright© Vicki Marie Riley 2021. All rights reserved.

BREAK THE LANGUAGE BARRIER LEVEL 4
WWW.ELPRINCIPECENTRE.COM
info@elprincipecentre.com

PRACTICE B: TRANSLATION

Carmen has toothache but she doesn´t want her boyfriend to know. She doesn´t want to go to see the dentist because she is scared, even though he is a nice man. In the end she can´t stand the pain any more and speaks to her brother Pepe. He says that it could be that the Chemists would have something to relieve the pain.

Carmen goes to the Chemist on the corner. It is quite full of people, and while the assistant serves them, Carmen looks at all the bottles and boxes on the counter looking for a remedy. Of course she doesn´t find it. She explains to the assistant her toothache and asks him for advice. He smiles.
"I can´t help you much. Its better that you go to the dentists as soon as possible. In the meantime you can buy aspirin to lessen the pain a little".

At the moment she is swallowing one her husband Robert enters the kitchen.
"What´s the matter that you are taking aspirin? If you have toothache, you know what you have to do. Tomorrow morning we are going to see the dentist."

The next day Carmen, accompanied by her husband, goes to see the dentist. She has turned pale andis trembling when she goes in the door. She doesn´t have to wait long before seeing the dentist, who examines her mouth very carefully and patiently.
"I´m afraid I can´t fill this tooth", he says, "I´m going to take it out, but it is important that you are not scared. I´m not going to hurt you."

When he has finished Carmen is very happy with the results. Now she doesn't have toothache.
"Thank you very much"- she says on leaving.
"You´re welcome", answers the dentist, "But if you don't want to return soon, it´s advisable that you don´t eat so many sweets. "

PRACTICE C:

1. ¿Por que no quiere ir Carmen al dentista?
2. ¿Por qué al final habla con su hermano Pepe?
3. ¿Qué dice Pepe?
4. ¿Dónde está la Farmacia?

Copyright© Vicki Marie Riley 2021. All rights reserved.

5. ¿Qué hace Carmen mientras el dependiente sirve a la gente?
6. ¿Qué consejo da?
7. ¿Quién entra en la cocina en el momento que está tragándose una pastilla?
8. ¿Qué dice?
9. ¿Cómo está Carmen cuando entra el el dentista?
10. ¿Tiene que esperar mucho?
11. ¿Puede empastar el diente?
12. ¿Qué va a hacer?
13. ¿Qué es importante?
14. ¿Cómo está Carmen cuando ha terminado y por qué?
15. ¿Qué es aconsejable según el dentista?
16. ¿Tienes miedo del dentista?
17. ¿Por qué?
18. ¿Cuándo fue la última vez que fuiste al dentista y que te hizo/ hicieron?

15. THE IMPERFECT SUBJUNCTIVE

PRACTICE A:

PONER 1.	2.	SER 1.	2.	ESTAR 1.	2.
pusiera	pusiese	fuera	fuese	estuviera	estuviese
pusieras	pusieses	fueras	fueses	estuvieras	estuvieses
pusiera	pusiese	fuera	fuese	estuviera	estuviese
pusiéramos	pusiésemos	fuéramos	fuésemos	estuviéramos	estuviésemos
pusierais	pusieseis	fuerais	fueseis	estuvierais	estuvieseis
pusieran	pusiesen	fueran	fuesen	estuvieran	estuviesen

HACER 1.	2.	ABRIR 1.	2.	SABER 1.	2.
hiciera	hiciese	abriera	abriese	supiera	supiese
hicieras	hicieses	abrieras	abrieses	supieras	supieses
hiciera	hiciese	abriera	abriese	supiera	supiese
hiciéramos	hiciésemos	abriéramos	abriésemos	supierámos	supiésemos
hicierais	hicieseis	abrierais	abriéseis	superiais	supieseis
hicieran	hiciesen	abrieran	abriesen	supieran	supiesen

BREAK THE LANGUAGE BARRIER LEVEL 4
WWW.ELPRINCIPECENTRE.COM
info@elprincipecentre.com

TENER 1.	2.	PENSAR 1.	2.	DECIR 1.	2.
tuviera	tuviese	pensara	pensase	dijera	dijiese
tuvieras	tuvieses	pensaras	pensases	dijeras	dijieses
tuviera	tuviese	pensara	pensase	dijera	dijiese
tuviéramos	tuviésemos	pensáramos	pensásemos	dijéramos	dijiésemos
tuvierais	tuvieseis	pensarais	pensaseis	dijerais	dijieseis
tuvieran	tuviesen	pensaran	pensasen	dijeran	dijiesen

PRACTICE B:

1. Quería que compraran la casa.
2. Era lástima que no pudieras venir a la fiesta.
3. No había nadie en el hotel que nos pudiera ayudar.
4. No creía que quisiera ir.
5. Dudaban/ dudaron que dijera la verdad.
6. Pidieron que cenáramos con ellos.
7. Limpió la casa antes de que llegara yo.
8. Fue/ Era probable que no terminaras.
9. No pensé/ pensaba que nadie me viera.
10. Fue/ Era terrible que estuvieran tan enfermos.
11. Quería que hablaran en español.
12. Esperábamos que no hubiera problema.
13. Esperaba que no estuvierais alli.
14. Dudaba que fuera la verdad.
15. No queríamos que supieras la verdad.

16. PRACTICE THE PAST SUBJUNCTIVE

1. ¿Esperabas que vivieras en España un día?
2. ¿Dudabas que Donald Trump ganara la elección?
3. ¿Fue una pena que Gran Bretaña saliera de Europa?
4. ¿No pensabas que hiciera tanto calor en España en el verano?
5. ¿Buscabas una casa que tuviera vista del mar la última vez que viniste a España?
6. ¿Era importante que aprendieras el subjuntivo?
7. ¿Aprendiste a conducir tan pronto como tuvieras bastante años?
8. ¿Preferías ir de vacaciones a un país dónde hiciera frio o calor?
9. ¿Ibas de restaurantes aunque fueran caros?
10. ¿Hacías mucho ejercicio los fines de semana aunque lloviera?

Copyright© Vicki Marie Riley 2021. All rights reserved.

11. ¿Te arrepentías estudiar Español después de encontraras el subjuntivo?
12. ¿Safricabas mucho para que tus hijos pudieron tener una vida buena?

FREE ANSWERS

17. VIAJE A ESPAÑA

PRACTICE A:

VERB	INFINITIVE	ENGLISH	TENSE	PERSON
1. es	ser	To be	present	3 p.s
2. hagas	hacer	To do/ make	subjunctive	2 p.s
3. dura	durar	To take/last	present	3 p.s
4. llegué	llegar	To arrive	preterite	1 p.s
5. estaba	estar	To be	imperfect	1 p.s
6. encuentro	encontrar	To find	present	1 p.s
7. dormir	dormir	To sleep	infinitive	
8. había pasado	pasar	To spend	past perfect	1 p.s
9. había querido	querer	To want	past perfect	3 p.s
10. quedara	quedar	To stay	past subj.	3 p.s
11. habían querido	querer	To want	past perfect	3 p.p
12. estuviese	estar	To be	past subj.	3 p.s
13. Resultaron	resultar	To result	preterite	3 p.p
14. intenté	intentar	To try	preterite	1 p.s
15. dormir	dormir	To sleep	infinitive	
16. Visitaba	visitar	To visit	imperfect	1 p.s
17. habían mandado	mandar	To send	past perfect	3 p.p
18. había tenido	tener	To have	past perfect	1 p.s
19. reservar	reservar	To reserve	infinitive	
20. tenía	tener	To have	imperfect	1 p.s

21. pudiera	poder	To be able	past subj.	3 p.s
22. ayudar	ayudar	To help	infinitive	
23. empecé	empezar	To start	preterite	1 p.s
24. preocupar	preocupar	To worry	infinitive	
25. quería	querer	To want	imperfect	1 p.s
26. llegara	llegar	To arrive	past subj.	3 p.s
27. acostarme	acostarse	To go to bed	imperfect	
28. eran	ser	To be	imperfect	3 p.p
29. Fue	ser	To be	preterite	3 p.s
30. me sentía	sentirse	To feel	imperfect	1 p.s
31. tenía	tener	To have	imperfect	1 p.s
32. estaba	estar	To be	imperfect	1 p.s
33. encontara	encontrar	To find	past subj	1 p.s

PRACTICE B:

The journey from London to Madrid is very long unless you make it by plane. In train and boat it takes more than thirty five hours. So, when I arrived in the train at Madrid's North Station I was very tired.

I always find it difficult to fall asleep on the train, and unfortunately I had spent the night before in a second class compartment with a French couple that had wanted the window to stay open. At the same time, some Spanish people, well dressed, had wanted it to be closed. This resulted in many arguments while I tried to sleep without success.

I was visiting Spain for the first time, and my bosses had sent me without warning. Therefore I had not had time to reserve a room in an hotel, nor did I have any address that could help me, and I started to get worried. I didn't want night to come without finding a place to sleep, and it was now five o'clock in the afternoon. It was a Sunday in winter and I felt a little lost and alone in that city so big and unfamiliar. But I had my mobile and credit card, and a few euros in cash, therefore I was convinced that I would find something.

PRACTICE B: FREE ANSWER

PRACTICE C:

1. ¿Cuánto tarda/ dura el viaje de Londrés a Madrid por tren y barco?
    Tarda/ dura mas de treinta y cinco horas.
2. ¿Cómo se sentía cuando llegó a la Estación del Norte de Madrid?
    Se sentía muy cansada.
3. ¿Por qué fue difícil dormir la noche antes?
    Porque había pasado la noche anterior en un compartimiento de segunda clase con otras personas.
4. ¿Por qué no había tenido ningún tiempo para reservar una habitación?
    Porque sus jefes le habían mandado sin aviso previo.
5. ¿Qué no quería?
    No quería que llegara la noche sin sitio para acostarse.
6. ¿Qué hora era?
    Eran las cinco de la tarde.
7. ¿Qué día fue?
    Fue domingo.
8. ¿Qué estación del año fue?
    Fue invierno.
9. ¿Cómo se sentía?
    Se sentía un poco perdido.
10. ¿Qué tenía?
    Tenía su móvil y tarjeta de crédito.
11. ¿De qué estaba convencido?
    Estaba convencido de que encontrara algo.
12. ¿Has estado en Madrid alguna vez? ¿Cómo era?
    FREE ANSWER

17. THE PAST SUBJUNCTIVE- "SER" AND "ESTAR"

PRACTICE A:

1. Manuel dijo que quizá sea médico un día.
2. Pensábamos que probablemente estuvieran allí ya.
3. Carmen nunca creía que estuviéramos felices para siempre.
4. Dudé que estuviera enfermo de verdad.
5. Esperabas que no viniera a la fiesta.
6. Cuando era joven esperaba que se casara con una chica simpaática.

7. Queríamos llevar el coche azul pero quizá estuviera roto.
8. Decidieron ir a la playa aunque estuvieron cansados.
9. Intenté llegar a la casa tan pronto come estuvieron listos.
10. ¿Comprastéis una casa tan pronto como tuvierais el dinero?
11. Sabía que a lo mejor no fuera un médico de verdad.
12. María pensaba que era una pena que fueran tan antipáticos.
13. No creíste que hubo nadie allí.
14. No creíamos que fueran sinceros.
15. Cuando Pablo tuvo el accidente no pensaba que nunca estuviera felíz de nuevo.

18. ONE SUNDAY MORNING

PRACTICE A:

VERB	INFINITIVE	SPANISH	TENSE	PERSON
1. was	To be	ser	imperfect	3 p.p
2. There was		haber	imperfect	3 p.s
3. were walking	To walk	caminar	imperfect	3 p.p
4. was running	To run	correr	imperfect	3 p.s
5. playing	To play	jugar	imperfect	3 p.s
6. was carrying	To carry	llevar	imperfect	3 p.s
7. were chatting	To chat	charlar	imperfect	3 p.p
8. laughing	To laugh	reirse	imperfect	3 p.p
9. stopped	To stop	pararse	preterite	3 p.s
10. asked	To ask for	preguntar	preterite	3 p.s
11. excuse	To excuse	disulpar	imperative	2 p.p
12. is	To be	estar	present	3 p.s
13. go	To go	ir	imperative	2 p.s
14. turn	To turn	girar	imperative	2 p.s
16. you will see	To see	ver	future	2 p.s
17. is	To be	ser	present	3 p.s

BREAK THE LANGUAGE BARRIER LEVEL 4
WWW.ELPRINCIPECENTRE.COM
info@elprincipecentre.com

18. explained	To explain	explicar	preterite	3 p.s
19. disagreed	To disagree	No estar de acuerdo	preterite	3 p.s
20. said	To say	decir	preterite	3 p.s
21. is	To be	estar	present	3 p.s
22. is	To be	ser	present	3 p.s
23. protested	To protest	protestar	preterite	3 p.s
24. are	To be	equivocarse	present	2 p.s
25. replied	To	contestar	preterite	3 p.s
26. continued	To continue	seguir	preterite	3 p.p
27. arguing	To argue	discutir	gerund	
28. got	To get (louder)	subir	preterite	3 p.p
29. became	To become	ponerse	preterite	3 p.p
30. lay down	To lie down	tumbarse	preterite	3 p.s
31. started	To start	arrancarse	preterite	3 p.s
32. stopped	To stop	pararse	preterite	3 p.s
33. could	To be able	poder	preterite	3 p.s
34. hear	To hear	oir	infinitive	
35. arguing	To argue	discutir	gerund	
36. had not realised	To realise	darse cuenta	Past perfect	3 p.p
37. he had gone	To go	ir	Past perfect	3 p.s
38. gave	To give	dar	preterite	3 p.s

PRACTICE B:

Eran las once un domingo por la mañana. Todavía hubo muy poco tráfico ní gente en la calle. Antonio y Carmen caminaban lentamente por lo largo de la acera. Delante de ellos su perrito Terri corría y jugaba. Antonio llevaba el periódico de domingo y charlaban y se reían. De repente un coche paró al lado de ellos. El conductor les preguntó:
"Disculpad, ¿dónde está el Ayuntamiento?

BREAK THE LANGUAGE BARRIER LEVEL 4
WWW.ELPRINCIPECENTRE.COM
info@elprincipecentre.com

"Ve todo recto, gira a la izquierda a la segunda calle, y verás el Ayuntamiento delante tuya. Es un edificio de ladrillos rojos..." explicó Carmen.

Pero Antonio no estuvo de acuerdo y dijo:

"Eso es el Centro de Salud. El Ayuntamiento está en la misma calle al final, a la derecha."

"No es verdad", protestó Carmen.

"Te equivocas", contestó Antonio.

Siguieron discutiendo, y sus voces subieron y subieron, y los insultos se pusieron más y más fuertes. Terrí se tumbó en la acera cansada con todos los gritos.

El coche se arrancó de nuevo y se paró cien metros más por alla, a un kiosco de periódicos. El conductor todavía pudo oír a Antonio y Carmen discutiendo- No se habían dado cuenta que se había ido ...

El hombre del kiosco le dio las direcciones correctas.

PRACTICE C:

1. ¿Qué día fue?
   Fue un domingo.
2. ¿Qué hora era?
   Eran las once.
3. ¿Hubo mucho tráfico en las calles?
   No, hubo muy poco.
4. ¿Qué hacían Antonio y Carmen?
   Caminaban por lo largo de la acera.
5. ¿Quién corría y jugaba?
   Su perrito Terri corría y jugaba.
6. ¿Qué llevaba Antonio?
   Llevaba el periódico de domingo.
7. ¿Qué pasó entonces?
   Un coche se paró al lado de ellos.
8. ¿Qué les preguntó?
   Les preguntó donde estaba el Ayuntamiento.
9. ¿Qué direcciones le dio Carmen?
   Le dijo ir todo recto, girar a derecha a la segunda calle y lo vería delante suyo.
10. ¿Por qué no estuvo Antonio de acuerdo?
    Porque dijo que eso era el Centro de Salud.
11. ¿Qué pasaron a sus voces y los insultos mientras siguieron discutiendo?
    Las voces subieron y los insultos se pusieron más fuertes.

Copyright© Vicki Marie Riley 2021. All rights reserved.

12. ¿Qué hizo Terri?
    Se tumbó en la acera.
13. ¿Qué hizo el coche?
    Se arrancó de nuevo.
14. ¿Qué todavía pudo oír el conductor?
    Pudo oírles discutiendo.
15. ¿Quién le dio las direcciones correctas?
    El hombre del kiosco le dio las direcciones correctas.

BREAK THE LANGUAGE BARRIER LEVEL 4
WWW.ELPRINCIPECENTRE.COM
info@elprincipecentre.com

19. VERB TABLES

1. LLEVAR-TO WEAR/CARRY/TAKE

PRESENT	PRESENT PERFECT	PRETERITE
llevo	he	llevé
llevas	has	llevaste
lleva	ha llevado	llevó
llevamos	hemos	llevamos
lleváis	habéis	llevasteis
llevan	han	llevaron

IMPERFECT	PAST PERFECT	FUTURE
llevaba	había	llevaré
llevabas	habías	llevarás
llevaba	había llevado	llevará
llevábamos	habíamos	llevaremos
llevabais	habíais	llevaréis
llevaban	habían	llevarán

CONDITIONAL	PRESENT SUBJUNCTIVE	PAST SUBJUNCTIVE
llevaría	lleve	llevara
llevarías	lleves	llevaras
llevaría	lleve	llevara
llevaríamos	llevemos	lleváramos
llevaríais	llevéis	llevarais
llevarían	lleven	llevaran

Copyright© Vicki Marie Riley 2021. All rights reserved.

2. APRENDER- To learn

PRESENT	PRESENT PERFECT	PRETERITE
aprendo	he	aprendí
aprendes	has	aprendiste
aprende	ha aprendido	aprendió
aprendemos	hemos	aprendimos
aprendéis	habéis	aprendisteis
aprenden	han	aprendieron

IMPERFECT	PAST PERFECT	FUTURE
aprendía	había	aprenderé
aprendíamos	habías	aprenderás
aprendía	había aprendido	aprenderá
aprendíamos	habíamos	aprenderemos
aprendíais	habíais	aprenderá
aprendían	habían	aprender

CONDITIONAL	PRESENT SUBJUNCTIVE	PAST SUBJUNCTIVE
aprendería	aprende	aprendiera
aprenderías	aprendes	aprendieras
aprendería	aprende	aprendiera
aprenderíamos	aprendemos	aprendiéramos
aprenderíais	aprendéis	aprendierais
aprenderían	aprenden	aprendieran

BREAK THE LANGUAGE BARRIER LEVEL 4
WWW.ELPRINCIPECENTRE.COM
info@elprincipecentre.com

3. ESCRIBIR- to write

PRESENT	PRESENT PERFECT	PRETERITE
escribo	he	escribí
escribes	has	escribiste
escribe	ha escrito	escribió
escribimos	hemos	escribimos
escribís	habéis	escribisteis
escriben	han	escribieron

IMPERFECT	PAST PERFECT	FUTURE
escribía	había	escribir
escribías	habías	escribir
escribía	había escrito	escribir
escribíamos	habíamos	escribir
escribíais	habíais	escribir
escribían	habían	escribir

CONDITIONAL	PRESENT SUBJUNCTIVE	PAST SUBJUNCTIVE
escribiría	escriba	escribiera
escribirías	escribas	escribieras
escribiría	escriba	escribiera
escribiríamos	escribamos	escribiéramos
escribiríais	escribáis	escribierais
escribirían	escriban	escribieran

Copyright© Vicki Marie Riley 2021. All rights reserved.

4, PODER- to be able

PRESENT	PRESENT PERFECT	PRETERITE
puedo	he	pude
puedes	has	pudiste
puede	ha podido	pudo
podemos	hemos	pudimos
podéis	habéis	pudisteis
pueden	han	pudieron

IMPERFECT	PAST PERFECT	FUTURE
podía	había	podré
podías	habías	podrás
podía	había podido	podrá
podíamos	habíamos	podremos
podíais	habíais	podráis
podían	habían	podrán

CONDITIONAL	PRESENT SUBJUNCTIVE	PAST SUBJUNCTIVE
podría	pueda	pudiera
podrías	puedas	pudieras
podría	puede	pudiera
podríamos	podamos	pudiéramos
podríais	podáis	pudierais
podrían	puedan	pudieran

BREAK THE LANGUAGE BARRIER LEVEL 4
WWW.ELPRINCIPECENTRE.COM
info@elprincipecentre.com

5. QUERER- to want/love

PRESENT	PRESENT PERFECT		PRETERITE
quiero	he		quise
quieres	has		quisiste
quiere	ha	querido	quiso
queremos	hemos		quisimos
queréis	habéis		quisisteis
quieren	han		quisieron

IMPERFECT	PAST PERFECT		FUTURE
quería	había		querré
querías	habías		querrás
quería	había	querido	querrá
queríamos	habíamos		querremos
queríais	habíais		querréis
querían	habían		querrán

CONDITIONAL	PRESENT SUBJUNCTIVE	PAST SUBJUNCTIVE
querría	quiera	quisiera
querrías	quieras	quisieras
querría	quiera	quisiera
querríamos	queramos	quisiéramos
querríais	queráis	quisierais
querrían	quieran	quisieran

Copyright© Vicki Marie Riley 2021. All rights reserved.

6. PEDIR - to request/ask for/ order

PRESENT	PRESENT PERFECT	PRETERITE
pido	he	pedí
pides	has	pediste
pide	ha pedido	pidió
pedimos	hemos	pedimos
pedís	habéis	pedisteis
piden	han	pidieron

IMPERFECT	PAST PERFECT	FUTURE
pedía	había	pediré
pedías	habías	pedirás
pedía	había pedido	pedirá
pedíamos	habíamos	pediremos
pedíais	habíais	pediréis
pedían	habían	pedirán

CONDITIONAL	PRESENT SUBJUNCTIVE	PAST SUBJUNCTIVE
pediría	pida	pidiera
pedirías	pidas	pidieras
pediría	pida	pidiera
pediríamos	pidamos	pidiéramos
pediríais	pidáis	pidierais
pedirían	piden	pidieran

7. TENER- To have

PRESENT	PRESENT PERFECT	PRETERITE
tengo	he	tuve
tienes	has	tuviste
tiene	ha tenido	tuvo
tenemos	hemos	tuvimos
tenéis	habéis	tuvisteis
tienen	han	tuvieron

IMPERFECT	PAST PERFECT	FUTURE
tenía	había	tendré
tenías	habías	tendrás
tenía	había tenido	tendrá
teníamos	habíamos	tendremos
teníais	habíais	tendréis
teníais	habían	tendrán

CONDITIONAL	PRESENT SUBJUNCTIVE	PAST SUBJUNCTIVE
tendría	tenga	tuviera
tendrías	tengas	tuvieramos
tendría	tenga	tuviera
tendríamos	tengamos	tuviéramos
tendríais	tengáis	tuvierais
tendríais	tengan	tuvieron

8. SER - To be

PRESENT	PRESENT PERFECT	PRETERITE
soy	he	fui
eres	has	fuiste
es	ha sido	fue
somos	hemos	fuimos
sois	habéis	fuisteis
son	han	fueron

IMPERFECT	PAST PERFECT	FUTURE
era	había	seré
eras	habías	serás
era	había sido	será
eramos	habíamos	seremos
eráis	habíais	seréis
eran	habían	serán

CONDITIONAL	PRESENT SUBJUNCTIVE	PAST SUBJUNCTIVE
sería	sea	fuera
serías	seas	fueras
sería	sea	fuera
seríamos	seamos	fuéramos
seríais	seáis	fuerais
serían	sean	fueran

9. ESTAR - to be

PRESENT	PRESENT PERFECT	PRETERITE
estoy	he	estuve
estás	has	estuviste
está	ha estado	estuvo
estamos	hemos	estuvimos
estáis	habéis	estuvistéis
están	han	estuvieron

IMPERFECT	PAST PERFECT	FUTURE
estaba	había	estaré
estabas	habías	estarás
estaba	había estado	estará
estabámos	habíamos	estaremos
estabais	habíais	estaráis
estaban	habían	estarán

CONDITIONAL	PRESENT SUBJUNCTIVE	PAST SUBJUNCTIVE
estaría	esté	estuviera
estarías	estés	estuvieras
estaría	esté	estuviera
estaríamos	estemos	estuviéramos
estaríais	estéis	estuvierais
estarían	estén	estuvieran

10. PONERSE - to put on/ to get

PRESENT	PRESENT PERFECT	PRETERITE
me pongo	me he	me puse
te pones	te has	te pusiste
se pone	se ha puesto	se puso
nos ponemos	nos hemos	nos pusimos
os ponéis	os habéis	os pusisteis
se ponen	se han	se pusieron

IMPERFECT	PAST PERFECT	FUTURE
me ponía	me había	me pondré
te ponías	te habías	te pondrás
se ponía	se había puesto	se pondrá
nos ponímaos	nos habíamos	nos pondremos
os ponías	os habíais	os pondréis
se ponían	se habían	se pondrán

CONDITIONAL	PRESENT SUBJUNCTIVE	PAST SUBJUNCTIVE
me pondría	me ponga	me pusiera
te pondrías	te pongas	te pusieras
se pondría	se ponga	se pusiera
nos pondríamos	nos pongamos	nos pusiéramos
os pondríais	os pongáis	os pusierais
se ponrían	se pongan	se pusieran

11. ACOSTARSE- To lie down/ go to bed

PRESENT	PRESENT PERFECT	PRETERITE
me acuesto	me he	me acosté
te acuestas	te has	te acostaste
Se acuesta	se ha acostado	se acostó
nos acostamos	nos hemos	nos acostamos
os acostáis	os habéis	os acostáis
se acuestan	se han	se acostaron

IMPERFECT	PAST PERFECT	FUTURE
me acostaba	me había	me acostaré
te acostabas	te habías	te acostarás
se acostaba	se había acostado	se acostará
nos acostábamos	nos habíamos	nos acostaremos
os ocostabais	os habíais	os acostaréis
se acostaban	se habían	se acostarán

CONDITIONAL	PRESENT SUBJUNCTIVE	PAST SUBJUNCTIVE
me acostaría	me acueste	me acostara
te acostarías	te acuestes	te acostaras
se acostaría	se acueste	se acostara
nos acostaríamos	nos acostemos	nos acostáramos
os acostaríais	os acostéis	os acostarais
se acostarçian	se acuesten	se acostaran

12. HACER - To do/make

PRESENT	PRESENT PERFECT	PRETERITE
hago	he	hice
haces	has	hiciste
hace	ha hecho	hizo
hacemos	hemos	hicimos
hacéis	habéis	hicisteis
hacen	han	hicieron

IMPERFECT	PAST PERFECT	FUTURE
hacía	había	haré
hacías	habías	harás
hacía	había hecho	hará
hacíamos	habíamos	haremos
hacíais	habíais	haréis
hacían	habían	harán

CONDITIONAL	PRESENT SUBJUNCTIVE	PAST SUBJUNCTIVE
haría	haga	hiciera
harías	hagas	hicieras
haría	haga	hiciera
haríamos	hagamos	hiciéramos
haríais	hagáis	hicierais
harían	hagan	hicieron

Copyright© Vicki Marie Riley 2021. All rights reserved.

BREAK THE LANGUAGE BARRIER LEVEL 4
WWW.ELPRINCIPECENTRE.COM
info@elprincipecentre.com

21. FINISH THE STORY- TERMINA LA HISTORIA

PRACTICE A: FREE ANSWERS: IF YOU WANT THEM CHECKED PLEASE SEND TO info@elprincipecentre.com 😊

22. ADJECTIVE PRONOUNS

1. QUALITATIVE -

PRACTICE A:

1. Él siempre compraba coches nuevos pero yo siempre compro (los) usados.
2. A ella prefiere (los) hombres bajos, pero a mí prefiero (los) altos.
3. Ellos querían la pregunta fácil pero queríamos el difícil.
4. Ella pensará que el rubio es guapo, pero yo preferiré el moreno.
5. La casa roja sería la suya (de él) y la blanca sería la suya (de ella).
6. Cada hombre quiere un coche de lujo pero siempre compran los económicos.
7. Siempre compraba una moqueta gris porque las blancas siempre ensuciaban.
8. Los dos vestidos son bonitos pero te gustará la corta más.
9. Él ha puesto las lámparas grandes en el salón y las pequeñas en el dormitorio.
10. La copa grande es para el vino tino y la pequeña es para el blanco.

2. QUANTATIVE NUMBERS AS ADJECTIVES.

PRACTICE B:

1. Algunos/as/unos/as
2. Las/los dos/ ambos/as
3. Cada uno/a
4. Demasiado/a
5. Los démas/ el resto
6. Los/las dos
7. La mayoria

8. menos
9. mucho/a/os/as
10. nada
11. ningún/o/a/os/as
12. el/ la/ otro/a
13. poco/a/os/as
14. (el/la) primero/a
15. Todo/o/a/os/as
16. (el/la/los/las) último/a/os/as
17. Unos/unas pocos/as
18. Varios/as

PRACTICE C:

1. Alguna gente vive/ algunas personas viven en la ciudad y alguna/algunas viven en el campo.
2. No podía decidir con que hermano casarme. Me gustaban los dos.
3. Nunca voy de copras con ella. Es peligroso, compra todo.
4. A Carmen le encantaban las fiestas. Siempre era la última para salir.
5. Mi marido le gusta la leche entonces compro mucha.
6. Mañana compraré algunos/unos libros españoles del centro comercial, te gustaría uno?
7. Anoche había muchos estudiantes en el bar. Cada uno bebió mucho.
8. Cada chica ha tenido un examen, pero varias no han aprobado.
9. Habrá mucha gente/ Habrán muchas personas en las tiendas pero poca/s en la playa.
10. Siempre comprábamos muchos regalos en Navidad, pero ahora no compramos ningunos.

3. UNSPECIFIED PEOPLE

PRACTICE D:

Alguien/nadie
Alguien/nadie
El/la que
Ellos/as que/ esos/as que/ los/ las que
El/la mayor/los/las mayores

El/la menor/los/ las menores
Nadie
Ningún/o/a
Todo/a/os/as/ todo el mundo

PRACTICE E:

1. A menudo el menor llevaba ropa usada.
2. Todos/todo el mundo pensaba que fue/era estupendo.
3. Alguien irá con ella al hospital.
4. Nadie va a decirle la verdad.
5. Nuestra clienta favorita es la que compra la ropa cara.
6. Hay muchas diferencias entre el niño mayor y el menor en la familia.
7. Oscar Wilde dijo que un cínico es él que sabe el precio de todo y el valor de nada.
8. Todos sufrirán/ todo el mundo sufrirá de vez en cuando, y la mayoría será más fuerte para la experiencia.
9. Todos estarán allí, pero algunos no conocerán a nadie.
10. Juan y Mateo viven el mismo apartamento, pero ninguno tiene televisión.
11. Alguien puede llevar esos pantalones.
12. Ramón ha dado consejo/s a todo el mundo.
13. Tendré una fiesta para mi cumpleaños. Alguien puede venir.
14. Para estos puestos. Los que/esos que trabajarán diez horas por día pueden pedir una entrevista.

4. UNSPECIFIED THINGS

PRACTICE F:

Algo
Cualquier/a
Lo/la mejor (cosa)
Lo/la mismo/misma (cosa)
Lo/la peor (cosa)
Nada

BREAK THE LANGUAGE BARRIER LEVEL 4
WWW.ELPRINCIPECENTRE.COM
info@elprincipecentre.com

PRACTICE G:

1. ¿Tienes algo para mi?
2. De todas las cosas en el mundo, la mejor es el amor.
3. No importó que llevé a su fiesta. Él siempre llevaba la misma cosa.
4. ¿Cuál quieren? Cualquier/a. No importa/da igual.
5. Fue estupendo cuando bailaron. El mejor fue cuando bailaron la salsa.
6. El servicio y el ambiente aquí son terribles. Pero la peor es la comida.
7. Nunca traían nada a la fiesta pero comía y bebía todo.
8. La peor cosa en una relación sería no poder confiar en la otra persona.
9. Habíamos pensado que era muy sabia, pero de hecho siempre dice la misma cosa.
10. No sé nada de esto.
11. Cualquier de estos coches sería bien para el invierno.
12. Estos libros son interesantes. He podido leer todos.
13. Cualquier de estos tres es perfecto.

PRACTICE H:

El letrero dijo: -Hoy es el primer día del resto de tu vida-
Si esto es verdad, entonces ¿que es mañana? El segundo? No puedo creer todo que leo. Nadie puede. Algunos creen todo. Alguna gente/ algunas personas creen en los anuncios en revistas. Supongo que algunos son de verdad pero la mayoría de estos anuncios son mentiras. Prometen todo y no entregan nada.

The sign said: "Today is the first day of the rest of your life". If this is true, then what is tomorrow? The second? I can´t believe everything that I read. No one can. Some believe everything. Some people believe the ads in magazines. I suppose that some of them are true but the majority of these ads are lies. They promise everything and deliver nothing.

BREAK THE LANGUAGE BARRIER LEVEL 4
WWW.ELPRINCIPECENTRE.COM
info@elprincipecentre.com

23. TRANSLATION ENGLISH TO SPANISH- THE GARDENER.

Practice A:

1. has been
2. went
3. to study
4. he left
5. is
6. is
7. tells
8. was
9. moved
10. had
11. had
12. lived
13. used to spend
14. watching
15. work
16. talking
17. I think
18. I learnt
19. realising
20. I know
21. I could
22. give
23. I went
24. was
25. I told
26. Was going to
27. Leave
28. Go back
29. Were
30. We had
31. They didn't speak
32. I knew
33. It was

Copyright© Vicki Marie Riley 2021. All rights reserved.

34. To continue
35. I started
36. I knew
37. I had made
38. I have enjoyed
39. Have learned
40. To accept
41. I do
42. They can
43. See
44. I am
45. Have found
46. To find
47. Are
48. To learn
49. Went
50. It makes
51. Respect
52. I help
53. Plam
54. They listen
55. I have
56. To say

Hugh Grantchester, 26, ha sido un jardinero por/durante cuatro años. Fue a la Universidad de Oxford para estudiar arqueología, pero lo dejó después de solo un trimestre. Su padre, Hector, es abogado, y su madre, Geraldine, es diseñadora. Hugo nos habla de su elección de carrera-

Cuando tenía 11, mudamos a una casa grande en Anglia del Este que tenía un jardín enorme. Teníamos un jardinero que vivía en una casita al final de nuestro jardín. Yo pasaba horas mirándole trabajar y hablando con él. Pienso que aprendí mucho sobre la jardinería sin darme cuenta. Un verano, cuando estaba todavía en la escuela, tuve un trabajo un centro de jardinería local y sabía todos los nombres de las plantas, entonces podía dar consejos a la gente.

Después fue la la Universidad y fue un disastre. Dijo a mis padres que iba a dejarlo y volver a trabajar en el Garden. Estaban furiosos. Tuvimos una discusión terrible y no me hablaron durante meses. Pero sabía que era/fue malgasto de tiempo seguir con la arqueología, y tan pronto come empecé la jardinería otra vez sabía que había hecho la decisión correcta.

He disfrutado cada momento de los últimos cuatro años y mis padres han aprendido aceptar que hago porque pueden ver que contento/felíz estoy y también porque muchos de mis amigos de la Universidad han encontrado difícil encontrar trabajos buenos. A veces la gente está sorprendida aprender que su jardinero fue a la Universidad, pero pienso que les hace respetar más a mi opinión. Les ayudo planear sus jardines y ellos escuchan lo que tengo a decir.

Practice B: Free answers

24. TRANSLATION ENGLISH TO SPANISH- THE COOK.

PRACTICA A:

1. has been
2. has
3. has lived
4. worked
5. is studying
6. tells
7. I think
8. I have always been interested
9. Lived
10. They had
11. She made
12. I used to love
13. Going down
14. Watching
15. She gave
16. I realized
17. I wanted
18. To be
19. I was
20. Chose
21. Chose
22. I had begun

BREAK THE LANGUAGE BARRIER LEVEL 4
WWW.ELPRINCIPECENTRE.COM
info@elprincipecentre.com

23. Had started
24. To make up
25. I knew
26. Would not approve
27. Cooking
28. I decided
29. To introduce
30. I told
31. I wanted
32. To do
33. Cookery
34. I went
35. I enjoyed
36. I know
37. I had to
38. Tell
39. I said
40. There was
41. Asked
42. Explained
43. Was
44. Painting
45. Writing
46. I could
47. See
48. Was
49. Didn´t get angry
50. Patted
51. Smiled
52. Kissed
53. I have opened
54. I think
55. They are
56. Is
57. He thinks
58. I am
59. Giving up
60. Farming

Copyright© Vicki Marie Riley 2021. All rights reserved.

BREAK THE LANGUAGE BARRIER LEVEL 4
WWW.ELPRINCIPECENTRE.COM
info@elprincipecentre.com

Giles Midmay, 24, ha sido cocinero profesional durante/ por tres años. Su padre tiene una granja grande en Devon. La familia ha vivido y trabajado en Devon durante/por más de tres cientos años. El hermano menor de Giles, Tobias, estudia Dirección de Granjas en la Universidad de Exeter. Giles nos cuenta/dice de su elección de carrera.

Pienso/ creo que siempre me ha interesado/ he tenido interés/ he estado interesado en la comida. Mis abuelos vivían en una casa enorme antigua en Lincolnshire y tenía una cocinera estupenda. Ella hacía comida tradicional estupenda inglesa. Me encantaba bajar a la cocina y mirarla trabajar, y me daba muchos consejos. Me di cuenta que quería ser cocinero cuando tenía mas o menos 12 años. Cuando los otros chicos elegían deporte en la escuela yo elegía cocinar. Con 15 años, había empezado hacer toda la cocina en casa para las cenas de mis padres y había empezado inventar mis propias recetas. Sabía que mis padres no aprovecharían de cocinar como profesión, entonces decidí presentarles la idea lentamente.

Les dije que quería a ver un curso de cocinar para la diversión, y fui a un hotel en Torquay durante un mes. Lo disfruté tanto, Sabía que tuve que decir mis padres entonces una noche durante la cena lo dije.

Primero había silencio. Entonces mi padre me preguntó ¿por qué? Expliqué que para mi cocinar era como pintar un cuadro o escribir un libro. Yo pude/podía ver que mi padre no estuvo/estaba feliz/contento pero no se enfadó. Me palmeó en el hombro y sonrió. Mi madre me sonrió. Y ahora que he abierto mi propio restaurante, pienso que están muy orgullosos de mí. Sin embargo, mi abuelo no es tan simpático, piensa que estoy loco para dejar la agricultura.

PRACTICE B:

1. ¿Cuánto tiempo ha vivido y trabajado la familia de Giles en Devon? Ha vivido y trabajado en Devon durante/por más de tres cientos años.
2. ¿Cuándo se dio cuenta que quería ser cocinero? Cuando tenía mas o menos 12 años.
3. ¿Por qué decidió presentar la idea lentamente a sus padres? Sabía que sus padres no aprovecharían de cocinar como profesión.
4. ¿Adónde fue para hacer un curso de cocinar? Fue a Torquay.
5. ¿Qué hicieron sus padres cuando les dijo? Primero había silencio. Entonces su padre le preguntó ¿por qué? Explicó que para él cocinar era como pintar un

cuadro o escribir un libro. Él pudo/podía ver que su padre no estuvo/estaba feliz/ contento pero no se enfadó. Le palmeó en el hombro y sonrió. Su madre le sonrió.

6. ¿Qué piensa su abuelo? Piensa que está loco para dejar la agricultura.
7. ¿Te gusta cocinar? **FREE ANSWER**
8. ¿Cuál/ qué es el mejor plato que cocines? **FREE ANSWER**

25. COMMON SPANISH VERBS THAT TAKE A PREPOSITION

PRACTICE A: (FREE ANSWERS)

1. ¿Te has acostumbrado a vivir en España?
2. ¿Qué has hecho para adaptarte a la vida aquí?
3. ¿Con quien puedes contar?
4. ¿Has aprendido a esquiar?
5. ¿Cuándo empezaste/comenzaste a aprender español?
6. ¿Te aburriste con tu último trabajo?
7. ¿Con qué te enfadas?
8. ¿Con qué tipo de persona te gustaría casarte?
9. ¿Con qué te preocupas?
10. ¿Con qué o quién sueñas?
11. ¿Te arrepientes salir del Reino Unido?
12. ¿Te cansas de aprender español?
13. ¿Qué piensas del gobierno Británico?
14. ¿Te olvidarás de español dentro de diez años?
15. ¿Alguna vez has consentido hace algo que no querías hacer?
16. ¿Estás listo/a para Navidad?
17. ¿Para qué trabajas?
18. ¿Quieres ir al bar/pub?
19. ¿Quién te cuida/cuida a ti?
20. ¿En quién confias?

26. ORDINAL NUMBERS.

PRACTICE A:

1. Yo vivía en la segunda casa a la derecha y Miguel vivía en la sexta.
2. No sé quien vive en la octava casa pero Carmen vive en la séptima.

BREAK THE LANGUAGE BARRIER LEVEL 4
WWW.ELPRINCIPECENTRE.COM
info@elprincipecentre.com

3. Mi coche es el tercero a la derecha y el coche de Pedro es el cuarto.
4. El biblio nos dice que Adan era la primera persona y Eva era la segunda.
5. Para mí, la primera película en una serie siempre será mejor que la segunda.
6. La tercera película de Tom Cruise fue/era mejor que su cuarta.
7. El quinto libro de Lee Child fue/ era más emocionante que el sexto, pero su séptimo fue/era el mejor de todo.
8. El primer día de la semana es lunes y el séptimo es domingo.
9. Agosto es el octavo mes, septiembre el noveno y octubre es el décimo.
10. La primera vez que fui a España fue mejor que el segundo, el tercero fue muy divertido pero el cuarto fue mi favorito.

PRACTICE B:

Cuando salíamos, mi mejor amigo y yo competimos para ver quien puede beber el más vodka. Per ejemplo, yo bebía uno y él bebía dos. Entonces yo bebía tres y él bebía cuatro. La primera persona para dejar/parar de beber fue el perdedor y ganó la otra persona.
La primera fue fácil. Y la segunda también. La tercera también fue buena. De la cuarta llegó a ser más difícil. La quinta fue un reto, también la sexta, la séptima y la octava. La novena siempre era una niebla; y yo nunca recordaba la décima!!

27. CONVERSATION PRACTICE-

PRACTICE A- FREE ANSWER- EXAMPLE BELOW

En el medico/centro de salud.

Doctor- Buenas días. ¿Qué/ cuál problema tienes/ hay?
Paciente- He tenido problemas en dormir y tengo un dolor de cabeza leve casi siempre. No tengo energía, y nunca quiero hacer nada.
Doctor- ¿Cuánto tiempo te has sentido así?
Paciente- Más o menos tres semanas.
Doctor- ¿Tomas algún medicamento? ¿Han sido cambios en tu estilo de vida? ¿Te preocupas por algo? ¿Tienes dolor de cabeza ahora mismo? ¿Bebes bastante agua? ¿Haces ejercicio? ¿Comes fruta y verdura?

Etc etc If you would like me to check your answer please send to info@elprinciecentre.com.

Copyright© Vicki Marie Riley 2021. All rights reserved.

28. LA GENERATION "DINK"

PRACTICE A:

A few years ago it was common to see the image of the classic couple surrounded by, at least, two children. Couples had to "tighten their belts" for the money to stretch and cover all the costs that a home represents. Nevertheless, current reality shows a different panorama of society. Modern couples have other worries between which children are not a relevant theme. These couples are known as "DINKS" (double income, no kids, or in Spanish - "doble sueldo, no niños").

These couples, (adults between 25 and 39 years old) keep busy planning their next holiday (they travel often). They keep up with the latest technologies, they visit luxury shops, dine in the most expensive restaurants and "of the latest fashion". Also they of course maintain an impeccable physical appearance, their image is a reflexion of success and advancement.

However. In conservative countries such as Mexico, Guatamala or Bolivia this concept is not very popular amongst older generations. They always ask the "DINKS"- When are you going to have children? Don´t you want to form a home/family? Or they recriminate them with the idea that "a happy marriage is a marriage with children". On their part, these couples live happily valuing everything that they can achieve when they invest their wages in things they could not have if they were parents.

For many people, this lifestyle of NO CHILDREN is selfish. For others is a new way of experimenting with freedom in all areas. It´s a fact that the generation DINK calls into question traditional roles of couples and makes us think about the direction the new society will take in the 21st Century.

And you? Are you a DINK?

www.ingramcontent.com/pod-product-compliance
Lightning Source LLC
Chambersburg PA
CBHW081347040426
42450CB00015B/3333